Saved from Enlightenment

Saved from Enlightenment

The Memoir of an Unlikely Devotee

TARINI BAULIYA

HOHM PRESS
Chino Valley, Arizona

Cover Design: Jacques Laliberte, Paulden, Arizona

Interior Design and Layout: Becky Fulker, Kubera Book Design, Prescott, Arizona

Library of Congress Cataloging-in-Publication Data

Bauliya, Tarini.
 Saved from enlightenment : the memoir of an unlikely devotee / Tarini Bauliya.
    pages cm
   ISBN 978-1-942493-07-5 (trade paper : alk. paper)
  1. Bauliya, Tarini. 2. Hohm Community--Biography. 3. Spiritual life--Hohm Community. I. Title.
   BP605.H58B385 2015
   299'.93--dc23
   [B]
                          2015023831

Hohm Press
P.O. Box 4410
Chino Valley, AZ 86323
800-381-2700
http://www.hohmpress.com

This book was printed in the U.S.A. on recycled, acid-free paper using soy ink.

To Lee Lozowick, the greatest devotee

Acknowledgments

*F*rom the conception of this book to its inking has been a nine-year pregnancy, complete with a team of people along the way who helped me finally deliver this book-baby. I mention some of you by name here because without you these stories would never have happened. If there should be any wisdom found in this book, I came by it because of you, by slipping on a banana peel, and by the masterful influence of my crazy-wise guru.

Nanci Healey, I hold you responsible for any courage I've mustered to dare the audacious in my life and for encouraging me to look beyond façades of beautiful stonework to the innards of things, accepting both the light and the dark, beautiful and not.

To my family, who have loved me in spite of my absenteeism, spiritual mumbo jumbo, and organic food snobbery: you teach me the impossible—humility.

Praise be to my editor, Regina Sara Ryan, my sister of sacred syntax and the Holy Mother of Death to the Darlings:

you cheerfully championed me through the mixed metaphors and the years.

My beloved sister-friends Linda, Shukyo and Nachama, you are the Ethels to my Lucy—each of you a clear light on real spirituality (authenticity and intrinsic dignity).

John and Capella Mann, I thank you for the magic of your friendship. I thank my sangha as well (too many I'd like to name), wherever and however you are today. Your perseverance through the heartbreak and wonders and whatevers of the path tethers me to practice.

As is my habit of saving the best bits to the last: Sam, I owe you some kind of wicked karmic debt for the gobsmacking awakening and selfless love that set this whole catastrophe in motion. And to the genetic gods I owe the fact that you inherited your father's IQ and not my gypsy genes or poor dental health!

My beloved Bruce, for your undying loyalty and adoration: you are the *great work* and love of my life, and the dog in my dharma!

Contents

Introduction

The room was bathed in a butter-tinted glow from the twinkling glass votive candles and bronze ghee lamps. The air was perfumed by exotic scents of sandalwood, jasmine and ylang-ylang. Long-stemmed roses and lilies in asymmetrical vases framed the dais where my guru sat cross-legged and draped in a birch-wood colored shawl that sat lopsided around his shoulders. I approached him, kneeled, handed him a single yellow rose and a book by David Sedaris titled *Me Talk Pretty One Day* with a note attached, then bowed my head to the floor at his feet, lingering there long enough to make a silent and earnest prayer for help to surrender.

The note I'd handed him was handwritten, informing him that the book I'd just offered, though he was not obligated to read it, was one of my favorites; and that, although I was not flattering myself at all, I would one day like to write in Sedaris's style and format, imagining short, candid, humorous essays about my life as a student in his (my guru's) school. It would be a hybrid, I explained, of Sedaris's book and *Rudi:*

14 Years with My Teacher, a contemporary spiritual classic by John Mann.

As I raised my head, my teacher leaned forward to hand me a Reese's Peanut Butter Cup (*prasad*, they call this ritual exchange of gifts between devotee and guru) and said, "If you write it, I'll publish it."

∾

Claustrophobic, in a passenger van circa *Chitty Chitty Bang Bang* not a year later, careening pell-mell through a hot dust bowl of a southern India town, a baker's dozen of us were swaddled and pinned in saris and dhotis, sweat soaked, with water bottles in a rainbow of colors slung over our shoulders—a conspicuous medley of Western devotees on pilgrimage. My guru, the master of ceremonies, was seated directly across from me, his voice booming above and through the chitty and bang bang: "Tarini, I want you to write . . . and don't hold . . . tell it like . . . you always do, and don't . . . punches . . . or your wicked humor," he said, as the cacophony of Indian traffic swallowed his words whole by twos and threes.

This was day fourteen in India. I looked and felt every bit the horse that had been ridden hard and put away wet. My senses were on overload, my mind a bowl of unfocused mush, and my nerves a jumble of exposed wires. Then, the sound of my guru's voice hollering—actually roaring—at me to "Write!" and "Tell it like it is, don't pull any punches, and don't lose your wicked sense of humor" jolted me, like the victim of a lightning strike now grounded to the earth.

I, being the good-doobie devotee, however, rallied quickly and applied the "when in Rome" adage, wagged a bobble-headed agreement, and gripped the seat beneath me with white knuckles as the bus driver raced and stopped and surged through a town that is an ink blot in my memory. Though the name and any distinguishing features of that particular town were swallowed up together with every other word my guru said in that sensory assault that was India, his message was delivered, and received.

◦∿◦

I was not then nor had I ever considered myself a writer. I wrote things, yes, but poorly. I was and am a dyslexic, untrained amateur who flattered herself by the mere thought that she would one day write a book the likes of David Sedaris's or John Mann's. Foolish enough to presume to write, and my guru the biggest Fool, who regularly, consistently, egged me on, our collusion against the odds has culminated in the book you now hold in your hands, dear reader.

This is no dharmic contribution to the annals of spiritual literature, nor a memoir of deep insight or religious intrigue. It is instead a heretical paean to my life on the spiritual path in the rare company of a crazy-ass, heretical spiritual master. It is a tribute to the context he held for my radical transformation, established in the ground of my being, which is love.

Forewarned is forearmed, as my guru was fond of saying.

Saved from Enlightenment

ONE

The Guru

> To relax is, of course, the first thing a dancer has
> to learn . . . It is the first thing any one has to learn
> in order to live. It is extremely difficult, because it
> means surrender, full surrender.
>
> —HENRY MILLER, *THE WISDOM OF THE HEART*

*N*ot all gurus are snake-oil salesmen, and
not all are pathological megalomaniacs; nor are they all jewels
of spiritual beauty in the crown of humanity. Be that as it may,
if you are anything like me, when you hear the word *guru* the
first thought that comes to mind is "gird your loins," followed
by recollections of turbans, tofu, sex scandals and Kool-Aid.
How'm I doing so far?

I do not come by the guru-devotee relationship naturally.
Hearing the word *guru* at one time sent up a flare in my mind:
a man (typically) preying on blind followers to relinquish
their good sense and independence, demanding that they

relinquish their personal power and turn over their paychecks to him (or her), the mortal beneath the turban. This skepticism runs in my family because (a) I am the daughter of the mother of all skeptics, with a loathing for authority figures; and (b) I was born into a bologna sandwich, Captain Crunch, vanilla ice cream clan, that named me Kristen, which translates as "Christ follower." And oh, there's the part about gurus having done their part to earn a seat at the sleazebag table, along with lawyers, politicians, and Wall Street bankers. On balance, this made meeting and eventually taking refuge in the guru a BFC (Big Fat Chance) and a tar baby.

A Sanskrit word, *guru* in its simplest understanding means "teacher." This translation is benign enough. But if, again like me, you still spasm at the sound of the seed syllables *gu* and *ru*, let's flesh out the origins of the word and confront our convulsive associations with it before we move on.

As a noun, *guru* more fully translates as "one who imparts knowledge." I can live with that. I've had several mentors in my life, as I'm sure you have, who have imparted their knowledge to me, and I was neither fleeced nor forced to trade tantric sexual favors for such gnosis. The adjectives "heavy" or "weighty," or to be more precise "weighty with spiritual knowledge," are part of its Sanskrit meaning. Since I'm not a dharma scholar nor a dharma savant, I turned to the *Guru Gita*, that ancient, bazillion-page song extolling the virtues of the guru, wherein I found the root *gu* to mean "beyond qualities" and *ru* to mean "devoid of form." I couldn't wrap my head around that, so I went to the Hindu sutras where I read that the guru is one who illuminates the darkness and dispels illusion, revealing ultimate Reality. Though this is clear enough, it's a bit woo-woo, so I then searched the more down-to-earth do's and don'ts of the Upanishads, in which I found something handy that I wish I'd known about years ago: a checklist to use to spot a true guru if you should ever be shopping for one. If, for example, you are by nature a "Mr. Grumpy Pants," don't be surprised by unwarranted joy or clarity of mind arising in a guru's presence. And—so say the Upanishads—your God-given talents may even volunteer themselves and blossom in the guru's proverbial garden.

By definition then, a guru does not emerge as a scam artist, nor does the guru necessarily warrant a retinal scan. So why *does* the guru give some of us the heebie-jeebies?

When I was in first grade, here in the States, I was taught to dutifully pledge allegiance to our flag and study the U.S. Constitution and the Bill of Rights; hence, I was immersed in the Western mantras of liberty, justice, and freedom for all. Couple this with the checkered history of some men and women who brought the guru-devotee relationship from the East (where the guru is as culturally ingrained as our liberty mantra is in the West) and doled out suspect knowledge of a spiritual or moral nature. As a Westerner, it's understandable that I might turn a skeptical eye on the guru.

∾

Human history tells a cautionary tale of the guru-devotee relationship. Every spiritual tradition, every great cause and tribal culture, has had their respective gurus—from Buddha, Christ, and Mohammed to the Dalai Lamas, to revolutionary leaders such as Gandhi, Mandela and King, to powerful shamans or wise elders. To these, many have entrusted their spiritual visioning and guidance. They have each left a legacy that has endured the tests of time. At the same time, however, humans have blindly followed such gurus, turning what is a wholly organic relationship of apprenticeship, or the transferring of spiritual lineages and inheritance, into a pathological state of dependency. What is worse, many have fallen prey to pathological gurus.

In a letter to my spiritual master, written eighteen years ago as I was beginning my apprenticeship in his school, I declared: "I'm drawn to the path for the clarity and authenticity—the fruits of practice I sense from many of your students. Though I'm having difficulty creating a distinction between you a man, a teacher, and the guru. Christ was my teacher, and I guess I could call him the first guru whom I worshiped. Struggling now to reconcile . . ."

His reply was part rudimentary instruction, part riddle: "Wasn't Christ a man?—Oh yeah, he's dead! . . . Don't fancy myself like JC—it'd swell me old 'ed big as a barn . . . By the way, you aren't 'worshiping' a man—that illusion must fall away. Keep on truckin' —Lee."

His note contained nary a breadcrumb of *what to do*, but only the statement of *what would become* an overarching context of my life with him through the years.

1. You are an intelligent adult.
2. Carve clear distinctions by doing your own work.
3. I'm not your savior, dad, lover, financial advisor, marriage-, career- or sex counselor.

❧

The moral to the tale of discerning the real from the counterfeit is "Buyer beware"; and, in this case, "Seeker beware." If it looks too good on the outside, it probably lacks inner substance. If the guru-teacher acts like a megalomaniac, he or she probably is.

A quote by the writer Hilary Mantel struck me as great wisdom regarding the guru-devotee relationship: "It is the absence of facts that frightens people: the gap you open, into which they pour their fears, fantasies and its desires." Although she wasn't referring to life on the path with a guru, her wisdom fits.

The guru gives us the heebie-jeebies not only because we have no context for such a role in our Western culture, but also because we hold our self-reliance as sacrosanct. A true guru, one who is the very absence of conventional reality with all its independence, certainty and facts, opens a breach so wide it requires a leap of faith and a shift in our reference point to the "other" if we hope to discover what exists beyond all our fears, fantasies and endless desires. It was the spiritual master Arnaud Desjardins who said, "The guru is not here to liberate us, but to help us understand it is the 'other' that liberates us."

As I write this, my guru has been dead nearly five years. When he was alive, he was the very predicament my spiritual well-being had been longing to encounter, in a form I could not have predicted: a pear-shaped, blue-eyed tar baby; a raspy old blues man; a Bad Poet; and a lover of God. Now that he is dead, I'm writing to reconcile that crazy mix and to carve a path out of "my own wilderness" (as Dani Shapiro so beautifully put it in her book on writing)—the wilderness of my fantasies of a guru as my savior, a father, a lover, or someone to make me special, if only by my claiming him as "my guru." I'm carving through my fears of belonging and, greater still, of something lacking in me.

And I'm bushwhacking through my endless desire for dazzling insights, bliss, and the hope of some ultimate truth to whack me on the head one day, only to come full circle as I stand in the gap that my guru was and ever will be, and take refuge there.

TWO

Not This—Not That!

We are all stumblers, and the beauty and meaning
of life are in the stumbling.

—DAVID BROOKS, *THE ROAD TO CHARACTER*

*B*ob Dylan's classic lyrics from "Love Minus
Zero" referring to his lady love, who reminds him that there is
no success quite like failure and that failure really is no success
at all, are a poetic description of the Sanskrit term *neti neti*—
"not this, and not that." To grok this crazy wisdom requires
curiosity and patience. The Advaita Vedantists call this practice
"inquiry": tedious questioning into the nature of all manifest
form to untangle the knot of what is *prior* to form, what is
not ultimate truth, and what *is* the essential nature of the
self. Dylan's muse strikes me as a woman of substance who,
consciously or not, knew a thing or two about this zigzag path
called *neti neti*.

Human birth is said to be the most auspicious of all births—a singularly rare shot at becoming a conscious being. From our first breath, we enter a divine process of growing old—a transformation that many a mystic has likened to the transformation of a caterpillar into a butterfly. If we are fortunate enough to make it to old age, we will have stepped cautiously or leaped courageously into the moments of our lives—tried and failed, loved and lost, given and taken, praised and raged—and each choice will have been an opportunity to transform our crude self into a dignified being as majestic as the monarch.

∾

It was Friday on a typical, sun-drenched day in late April 1974. My best friend Jayne and I concocted a plan during first period to skip school that afternoon and ditch to the beach to get a jump start on our summer tans. The plan: in the hurly-burly of kids slamming lockers and migrating in flocks to the lunch quad, we'd make our move.

Ring! The siren of the lunch bell echoed through the halls and caromed off the sun-bleached wood and stucco walls of the buildings, signaling our nonchalant slip to the football bleachers, where we met, drifted past track and field practice, and exited the gate onto St. Anne's Drive. Sea salt, eucalyptus, jasmine and oleander scented the air, their sweet perfume following us onto Thalia Street to the *Have'a Chip* stand. We dropped our book bags to the pavement and plopped down in the curbside seating area underneath the palm-thatched awning of the twenty-by-twenty-foot shack.

As Jayne and I waited, brimming with freshman-girl anticipation for our chips and guacamole, the familiar sound of the Hare Krishna chant rose and fell in crescendo with the surging traffic along the Pacific Coast Highway. Just across the street, at the corner of Thalia and the PCH, I located the Indian sect undulating in swirls of Orangesicle-colored sheeting. The signature scent of Nag Champa mixed with patchouli and curry wafted toward us, mingled with the salty spray of the waves that crashed just a block from the intersection. Tulsi beads plunged and swayed from the chanters' necklines, while shaved heads—save for the freakish scraggle of hair dangling from the occipital bone, the way an unkempt tail sways from the smooth sheen of a horse's rump—glistened in the coastal sunlight. Then we fixed upon the enigmatic cotton bag that hung from each of the chanters' wrists resembling the passive feedbag that hangs from a horse's mouth. Waiting for my chips and guac, I perched my chin atop my upturned palm as I gazed in fascination at their exotic Indian dancing, the fingers of my other hand drumming an absentminded rhythm to their call-and-response chant.

I noticed Jayne's inquiring eyes following mine, then slicing quickly back to fix on me. With the sleek slope of her bronze shoulders hunched over her folded arms, she leaned within inches of my face and asked, "What are those totally weird bags they wear over their hands?"

"Huh? I know! Like, they're totally creepy, aren't they?"

"Uh-huh . . . and gross!" Jayne said, as if diagnosing cancer with the authority of an oncologist.

"I dunno. Maybe they have a hand deformity and they wear those gross bags so they don't freak people out when they chant in public," I said.

"They totally freak people out, with or without the hand deformity bag, ya-geek!" Jayne countered.

Just then we heard our names called, announcing that our order was ready. I sprang from my seat like Olive Oyl, limby and blithe, as Jayne glided, shapely and confident, from hers. Collecting our food, we slung our book bags over our shoulders and made our way to the crosswalk directly past the Indian melee. As we waited for the light to turn green, savoring our first bites of the nirvanic bliss, I averted eye contact with the sect but stole a close-up peek at the cloaked claws bent inside the mysterious bags, as if spying on a leper colony.

"Grace, come on. Green means *let's go!*" Jayne jolted me from my trance with her nickname for me—"Grace," an equal balance of endearment and ironic reference to my gangly clumsiness. Then, with a twitch of her head, she directed me to the crosswalk while the Hare Krishna chant surged above the hum of idling traffic: "Hare-Rama/Hare-Rama/Rama-Ram-a."

I spent my formative years and came of age in the sixties and seventies in Laguna Beach, California—white as sun-bleached driftwood, a middle-class born-again Christian. Laguna was the Bohemia of the many beach towns that form the jagged spine of the Southern California coastline, a haven to hippie, artist, writer, poet, actor, and grifter-surfer. Even the peace-and-love-promoting surfing band known as the Brotherhood of Eternal Love, made infamous by the LSD guru Timothy Leary, settled in Laguna's preternatural beauty and countercultural milieu.

The Hare Krishna movement, the one George Harrison thrust into the limelight with his multiplatinum song "My Sweet Lord," found sanctuary in the ecumenical arms of Laguna, too. As a born-again, I was intimate with Pentecost, falling gravitationally into a devotional relationship with Christ as though I'd been Magdalene or a gospel singer in a past life. Growing up in Laguna and crossing paths with Krishna devotees milling, chanting, and beating drums as their heads swooned and their eyes lolled with a Stevie Wonder gospel groove, I was too fearful to admit that their devotion struck a chord in me. My wide-eyed curiosity tugged at me to join the chant, which looked and sounded an awful lot like being slain by the Holy Spirit and speaking in tongues!

It took me years and many hours of therapy to free myself from fears of devil possession and from the tyranny of an alcoholic father who, by self appointment, was the household authority and moral compass. In time, my innate curiosity, wisdom beyond my years, and a genetic pull to know God was triumphant. When the time came to come of age and explore new rooms of my consciousness, I shied from my hometown's mascot drug, LSD, and from joining the Hare Krishna cult, opting instead for weed, psilocybin-rich fungi, copious amounts of tequila, and a wanderlust for God—albeit a god from another country, like India and Africa and Tibet for starters—a god who didn't speak King James English and wasn't hung up on throwing kind, decent, human beings into the fiery abyss.

The music of the seventies turned my whole bohemian, born-again, Krishna-chanting, tyrannized mix into a symbiotic mash up and awakening. Crosby, Stills, Nash & Young, The Stones, Jackson Brown, Sweet Baby James, Bonnie Raitt, Dylan, Supertramp, Jimi Hendrix, and George "My Sweet Lord" Harrison played like a soundtrack at the coming-out party for my devotion. The mix and the mood was awakening something in me and moving me to ask the deeper questions: Who am I? Who and what is God? And why am I here?

∾

Following my coming-of-age era . . . let's skip forward to the first half of my twenties in the midst of a cultural phenomenon that I refer to as The Debauched Period of Disco. I've worked hard to block this period from my consciousness, so you'll forgive me if my memories are wee cryptic. Think cocaine, drinking, and a dog's breakfast of men, culminating in my first marriage, followed by its messy divorce and a now three-year-old son, his tiny and trusting palm clutching the unraveling hem of my life.

"We can run but we cannot hide." Somebody said this. I don't know who and I don't know why, but I'm in agreement. The hounds of life will track us down and, when they eventually find us, will drag us back to their master. Then, if not dead yet, we'll be begging for mercy. There is perhaps no single event in one's lifetime that will drop us to bended knee, begging for mercy with heart rent and our big ideas blown to smithereens, as will having a child. My son Sam broke open what had become my very lost, lonely, and insecure heart in such a way that only a god (male, female or androgynous) could possibly heal.

THREE

Birth Events

Lo I am with you always means when
you look for God,
God is in the look of your eyes,
in the thought of looking,
nearer to you than your self,
or things that have happened to you.
There's no need to go outside.

Be melting snow.
Wash yourself of yourself.
—JALĀL AD-DĪN RŪMĪ, TRANSLATION BY COLEMAN BARKS

"*I*f you were my wife I'd be prepping you
for a C-section right now" my ob-gyn said with the conviction
of a Jesuit. I was eight hours into transitional labor and repeating my natural-childbirth mantra: "Welcoming, receiving, and
please Baby Jesus or Holy Trinity give my son all his fingers
and toes and spare him orthodontics!" I had my Lamaze and

La Leche League classes under my belt, my copy of *What to Expect When You Are Expecting* bathed in soft light on my bedside table, and Windham Hills's *Winter Solstice* playing ambient and serene from a tape recorder provided by the birthing center of the Yavapai Regional Medical Center. Before my doctor could offer a medical reason why my cervix was not as wide as the Grand Canyon, I said, "You should be able to drive a truck through there by now. What gives?"

"Not your cervix," he said, apparently nonplussed.

"No shit, Sherlock!" I shot back.

My doctor raised his kind brows above the rim of his magnifying goggles, cutting a look between the V of my spread knees that said all I needed to know. You know that look on a mother's face, four kids dangling like possums from the cart in the grocery store as they wear down her last nerve? That look that says: "You kids utter one more word and I'll give you away to that old man driving that electric scooter and wearing a bib!"

"Send in the spinal tap guy," I said to my kind doctor, defeat darkening my face.

In sixty seconds or less, doctors and nurses materialized and descended on me with the stealth of the undead on a warm mammal. Spooky fast they washed, shaved, catheterized, and injected me with lidocaine as oxygen hissed through tubes taped to my nostrils, and Sam's heartbeat (we were already on a first-name basis) drove a bass rhythm through fetal speakers connected to my cervix that made my heart hurt.

In the next sixty seconds, a new team of nurses cantilevered me onto a gurney. The nurse chosen to maneuver the gurney into surgery lurched me out into the hall and down a blur of beige corridors that led to the operating room. As she navigated each turn, it felt as if she had lost control of a fighter jet and was attempting to pull it from a dead fall at Mach 4. Banking off walls, she sped forward, with me in the middle of contractions that gripped my abdomen in ten-second intervals with a force that was capable of ejecting a bowling ball from a syringe.

Arriving at last in the operating room, I was introduced to the anesthesiologist—again. (He'd apparently been one of the stealthy undead who prepared me for the ride to surgery.) Covered head to toe in surgical cap and gown, his John-Lennon glasses filled by round, serene blue eyes that appeared to have been custom-fit to his frames, he peered into the pond of my quaking face, placed a reassuring hand on my shoulder, and said, "Hi, how ya' feelin'?"

"Like an alien has abducted my abdomen," I said. "But I can still feel my toes. Do you have anything stronger for the pain?" I searched the kind orbs of his eyes for signs of hope.

"I'm going to give you an epidural," he said. "This is an anesthesia I will inject into your spine. You'll be numb from the waist down in a matter of minutes. I need you to roll over on your side and hold very, very still."

"Give me your best shot, Doc," I said. "And can you work your magic in ten seconds or less, before the next contraction? Otherwise, all bets are off on the 'very still' part." Then I rolled to my side, clutched my husband's outstretched hand, turned to meet his gaze, and noticed that a disturbing resemblance to Munch's *The Scream* had come over his otherwise sweet face . . . though I knew this was *not* the look he was after.

Inside of twenty minutes on April 15, 1988, Sam, covered in a green film, was successfully removed from the cocoon of my abdomen. God bless his little heart, he was so stressed out from banging his head against the vault of my cervix that he had his first baby poop while the team of doctors raced to get him out. This accidental poop in utero had the effect of the BP oil spill on a baby sea turtle, beached and gasping for air. My doctor held the little green face inches from mine for a sneak peek and said, "Mom, say hello to Sam!"

"Hi, Sam. Do you like green eggs and ham?" Though my first words to Sam were a terribly unoriginal reference that Sam would come to suffer good-naturedly over the years, they were the first that came to mind in my drugged and oxytocin-euphoric state.

Just as I was falling head over heels in googly-eyed love with Sam, a nurse whisked him away with the precision of an Indy pit crewman, transferring him to an incubator that resembled a NASA spacecraft, where he would spend the first forty-eight hours of his life with his little lungs working overtime dredging up toxic poop while he learned to breathe.

Those hours were infinity long. I came down from my cocktail of drugs in existential fear that the god of my born-again youth was tapping his omnipresent, self-righteous finger on the table at me and, in an annoying-as-hell tone, saying, "No more shenanigans, young lady!" As for Jesus, baby or resurrected, he was MIA. I can hardly watch Benicio del Toro in that bathtub scene in *Fear and Loathing in Las Vegas* without chilling flashbacks of those two days in the hospital as Sam fought the odds to make his way into this world. I spent forty-eight hours soaking in the bathtub of abject fear and loathing, beginning with the conviction of having failed my first test of motherhood—natural childbirth, which all good and selfless moms do! It was official. I was an urchin, not a mother. A spineless invertebrate. A reprobate who ought not to have reproduced. And now I was hopelessly, googly-eyed in love with little Yertle the Turtle.

I know I am not alone in this chamber of heartbreak that is childbirth and that I share a version of the enlightening event with nearly every mother dating back to Cro-Magnon mom. My realization, over twenty-six years of experience since that day, is that few shocks in life are capable of snapping us out of the hallucination (if only temporarily) that we are all blissfully drunk on: that we are all unique somebodies, special from all other carbon-based matter. The instant I looked into the ancient lakes of Sam's newborn eyes, the gig was up. Imagine first looking at Orion's Belt with the naked eye and then observing it through a high-powered scope that reveals vast horizons and unseen worlds within worlds. We stutter and stumble, asking, "Who knew?" The day Sam was born, as I gazed adoringly at him, the silk of his cheek pressed to the center of my chest, his puny hand tucked in mine, time was arrested. Self-identity merged with other. Love suffused every atom of being: him, me, my husband, nurses. I lost all concern that my hospital gown had no back. The cosmic joke was exposed: we are all one.

On that day, I knew without a doubt that we are infinitesimal parts of a never-ending, unspeakable love—a generative goodness and divinity: beauty we originate from and unite in, and one day return to. No drug, no orgasm, neither Beethoven's *Ninth Symphony*, "My Sweet Lord," nor Jimi Hendrix's "Voodoo Child" or Stevie Ray Vaughn's "Voodoo Chile" had ever been sufficient to crash the www.me.com of Me. But the shock of this pure, precious beauty in my arms dismantled that delusion with such gobsmacking force that it rocked the foundation of my whole hallucinatory narrative of separation off its axis, and I was toast.

Sam's birth marked the moment when beauty and love exposed the flimsy veil of the grand illusion, and although

I do not know the full gift of that shimmering instant, it exposed me to the knowledge that serving the other is the doorway to grace, and to loving God. A few years later, I was ready for a reminder.

∽

"You know what you need?" he said. "You need to find God and serve something greater than yourself." The arrow of his words coursed through the fifty feet between us and landed dead center in the bull's-eye of the nameless, aching need inside me. All the bodies in the room swung round, and eighteen sets of eyes tracked on me. Jim, the messenger, stood defenseless—arms slack against his sides, the coals of his dark eyes flickering with sincerity.

The features of the rented community center in Sedona, Arizona, faded from my view that day in 1993 as the eighteen others attending the workshop fell mute in a meditative silence. I felt as bare-assed as the legendary emperor, and with knee-jerk snark—in an effort to cover up—I took aim at the messenger. "Well, *I* don't *have* a guru like you do, Jim," I said. "And last time I checked, *my* teacher was crucified a couple hundred years ago, so I'm fresh out of candidates."

Jim was both the facilitator and founder of the transformational workshop called The Event that I'd been attending. A commanding six-foot-five-ish whooping crane of a man with the gait of Gumby, Jim spoke with the particular authority of one who'd done his time in psychoanalysis. For the past twenty-five years he'd also been a student of a spiritual master in a school of traditional practices rooted in both the Hindu and Buddhist traditions. And it was here, in this meeting, that the influence of his spiritual master, his *guru* (if you'll pardon the expression), would begin to inform and positively influence the course of my own life.

Although Jim's study of these great spiritual traditions and years of devotion to his teacher informed the workshop with context, The Event was not overtly spiritual in nature, nor was it a study of these traditions. It was, in fact, adapted from a program that originated in prisons with hardened criminals and was designed to break through the crystallized defenses—the "act" Jim called it—and the "life script" that set one on a career course in criminal behaviors.

This particular Event in Sedona in 1993 was not my first—nor was I a stranger to being cornered by Jim's assertions—but I was a fugitive from the law of averages that day. I was an Event regular, doing my New-Age best not to repeat the mess I'd made of my marriage, and working to reassure myself that I was not "Mommy Dearest" turning my toddler son into the next Unabomber. I was in the midst of a Chernobylean meltdown during those first years after Sam was born, biting my nails to the cuticle and pacing worse than Dustin Hoffman's *Rain Man* jonesin' for Judge Wapner! I was desperately seeking substance—some core strength of being, perhaps—and desperate to become the other functional half of the parenting team for Sam, as my ex-husband was stacking up to be. In the closet of my private thoughts, my greatest fear was that I was profoundly superficial. I had no distinguishing character traits such as self-respect, self-sacrifice, integrity—genetic or inbred—that I fantasized *real* parents passed to their children as readily as passing the salt and pepper. All I had to pass on to Sam was an insatiable need for approval, a California beach-girl vanity, ruined credit, and poor dental health. Or so I felt.

During the enrollment process for my first Event I had queried Jim on the program's hailing from the prison system with a wise crack: "Divorce is not a felony, last time I checked, is it?"

"True," he answered, as if to say *"Touché!"* then countered, "And yet, like criminals, whose behaviors are outside their awareness to such a degree that they land in prison repeatedly, without awareness of our behaviors we too are destined to repeat damaging patterns; then we wonder why our lives are unfulfilled, and why we feel stuck in a prison . . . of our own making."

"Right—yeah, uh-huh."

"We marry, divorce, have children, get into a new relationship and start the pattern over again. This may be the perfect time for you to examine how you got here, and maybe gain some awareness about it so you don't repeat the pattern. Don't you think?"

I knew enough psychological jargon—having done time in Adult Children of Alcoholics and carrying an impressive bibliography of self-help books read and a resume of workshops attended—to be obnoxious! The Event was sounding more and more like it might just help me snap back from this divorce, feel like myself again, and get on with my life as a single, aware mom. "Sign me up," I said.

My fantasy about the weekend ahead was that it would be all gestalty. We'd sit in a circle, share our feelings in an AA sort of way and, short of singing "Kumbaya," confess we needed help from our fellow Eventers. We would find our power, and then *Shazam*, I would be Nelson Mandela–deep, having rid myself of the mantle of guilt I'd been schlepping around for leaving a perfectly loving husband and father, even as our three-year-old son dangled from the window of my self-esteem issues.

∾

My first Event kicked off on a brisk Friday evening in February of 1991, in Prescott, Arizona. The evening was a "what to expect" for the two days that would follow, along with a layout of the rules. Jim gave the introduction, which turned out to be an embellishment on the theme he had used to enroll me in the weekend, adding that all that was expected of us was to "Participate, and show up for 'the game,'" as he called it. Then, drawing from a code-of-honor-among-thieves thing, he announced *The Rules*: "There are only two," he said, serious as a Hell's Angels leader, as he scratched them in bold print on a white easel with black Magic Marker:

1. No violence.
2. No leaving.

Surprised, I took in a gulp of air.

"No matter how uncomfortable you get, no matter how angry you may feel during the weekend, does everyone agree to rule #1, no violence?" Jim asked with a razor-straight face. He scanned the room making eye contact with each of the twenty participants to lock in our agreement. "No matter how uncomfortable you get—no matter what another person says to you during the weekend—does everyone agree to rule #2, no leaving? You all agree to complete the weekend?" Again Jim obtained agreement from each of us, somewhat like an airline attendant extracting a verbal "yes" from exit-row passengers confirming that, in trade for the privilege of three extra inches of leg room, they were willing and able to deploy the exit door and assist others in the event the plane plummeted from thirty thousand feet in a crash landing.

The chill that ran down my spine formed icebergs of my cold feet. No violence and no leaving? Of the list of possible rules defining the boundaries for the weekend, these two were *it* in a nutshell? Jim and Stan, his co-facilitator, proceeded to explain a process called "stalking," which we would all be doing throughout the gig. Stalking, paired with The Rules, should have been a news flash that finding my inner Nelson Mandela was going to be a manhunt led by bounty hunters.

The next morning I arrived on time at the rented, turn-of-the-century loft in a historic bank building in downtown Prescott, where we had gathered the night before. Twenty metal chairs were formed neatly into a circle, and each of the participants chose a seat (so far, so good). Jim kicked off the morning session by chatting up an Eager-Beaver man. In sixty seconds of conversation, Jim summed up the man's "act." Was this stalking, I wondered? I watched and listened intently, sizing up the process to get the hang of it. To my horrified eyes and seared ears, stalking as it continued left me with the same uncomfortable, conflicted feelings I have about eating lobster. If you're a crustacean lover (as I am), the mere mention of this tender, butter-basted, transcendental delicacy produces salivary effects. Lobster is the food of the gods! But then there is the matter of *cooking* the lobster. Forty-five to fifty seconds, they say: the time it takes for the creatures to scald, squirm and thrash—some even say "cry"—before they die. How much conscious awareness can a person stomach?

As the pace of The Event quickened, Jim and Stan stalked Eager-Beaver man further about what they had identified as his Mama's-Boy act. "How's that working for you?" Jim asked him. Without warning, a Rescuer Girl babbled a naive attempt to save Mama's Boy from the maw of their facilitator skill. With what appeared to be signs of ADD, Jim and Stan lost interest in Mama's Boy, abandoning him as if screeching away from a drive-by shooting, and turned their full attention on good little Rescuer Girl.

"Wow! That's interesting. What's that about?" Jim said, his neck craning to face her while the length of his body wheeled around in what seemed like single-frame animation. Startled by the shift of attention, every eye in the room bounced to good little Rescuer Girl the way eyes track a Wimbledon tennis match to keep up with the speed and proficiency of the game.

"What? What's *what* about?" she said, her naiveté on parade as she withered in defense, all eyes laser fixed on her.

"How come ya need to rescue 'im? He did'n invite yur help," Stan said, drawing slow on his vowels, giving a nod to Greg Allman. Stan was a lead singer and guitar player in a rock band, and he looked the part: slight and wiry, with dark-brown hair groomed into a ponytail-mustache-beard combo that framed his features and was tied together with a Jesus bow. Stan was easy on the ear and eye, which was troubling, since he was Jack-Nicholson-*Shining*-intense and wound tight as the strings on his guitar.

"Yeah, we're all adults here. Everyone can take care of themselves, and none of us are going to need your sympathy," Chip-on-the-Shoulder Guy announced, speaking up for the first time, with an authority that handed permission slips to anyone else with an opinion.

The morning unpacked one well-developed story after another, each participant revealing himself or herself without the use of a Myers-Briggs test. As the neon from one individual's story flickered across the room, Jim and Stan gravitated to the flashing sign with trained instinct. Strategies created to play safe, play the victim, get needs met, get attention, be right—whatever covers the ego had scripted were eventually blown.

By lunchtime of day one I had managed to avoid being stalked but was so freaked that I resolved to get the hell out before they were onto me, protesting to myself, "These people are bat-shit crazy. To hell with agreements, I'm outta here after lunch!" Too insecure and concerned with the opinions of others to leave by myself, at lunch I cornered Deer-in-the-Headlights Woman seeking approval and, with malice, over soup and salad enrolled her to mount a small coup. "Jim could have escaped from a penitentiary for the criminally insane, for Pete's sake—and The Event *was* designed in prison!" I said, focusing on the whites of her eyes as I spoke.

"I'm not comfortable with this stalking stuff, either; it's borderline abusive," Headlights Woman said.

"You're right! Who knows what this lunatic is really up to?" I affirmed, angling for solidarity.

The group reconvened in the loft after lunch, promptly at 1 PM. The circle of chairs had been straightened with Zen attention to detail, and the high afternoon sun washed the space in warm light, sending the shadows to cower in the corners. We resumed our seats.

Just as my lips quivered apart to form my announcement that "I and Deer-in-the-Headlights Woman have decided y'all are criminally insane, and we're leaving before you start passing the Dixie cups filled with lithium," Jim beat me to the punch and opened season on me.

"So, Ms. Perfect, what's *your* story?" he said, leaning forward to rest his elbows on the cliff of his knees. I followed the dark beads of his narrow-set eyes, now glaring directly at me from beneath a mantle of rumpled eyebrows.

"What do you mean by 'Ms. Perfect'? I'm not acting as if I'm perfect," I said, my lip twitching, my shoulders squaring into a protective armor.

"Ree-ly?" he said.

"No . . . I don't . . . I don't think I'm perfect!"

"Oh, that's interesting," he said as he stood, the tails of his pressed button-down shirt draping over the lap of his designer jeans. In Qigong slow motion, with the measured steps of a heron fishing for a meal, he crossed the circle and approached me. As though Jim secreted a pheromone with an imperceptible tilt of his head, the person next to me evacuated her seat like a crab discarding its shell. Jim lowered his towering frame to the now-vacant chair, swung his right leg over his left, and leaned back, draping his lanky body into a *Cool Hand Luke* slouch. "That's interesting, because you've managed to play it perfectly safe, barely saying a word all morning," he said. "Perfectly self-righteous in your opinions about what you think is going on here," he continued, his taut upper lip stretching across his narrow smile, forming a smirk that pumped unpredictability into the tank of his eyes.

Sweat beads pooled in every fold of my body, from my eyelids to my toe jams. My sympathetic nervous system kicked into hyperdrive as my adrenal glands leaked fight-or-flight messages across enemy lines, signaling my brain chemistry to either prepare for war or run the f*** away! A gush of unbidden anger responded *Fight*! but I hesitated for a fraction of a second to calculate my next move. With cunning, Jim seized on the moment and leaned in, his body language shifting to engage. "Your clothes are perfect, your hair is perfect, and your Ice Woman act is lookin' good and goin' nowhere. What's it about?"

"Who made *you* the authority on us all, Mr. Designer Jeans?" I said, lamely. I felt dizzy. Like I might need medical attention. The room was closing in on me, and I was having a hard time focusing as I reeled from the Ice-Woman jab.

There are events in each of our lives that carve a fork in the road—moments when distinct, equitable choices point in different directions and we choose a path that shapes an entire era. And, there are those moments where shit happens so fast we're lucky if we have time to tie our running shoes. What occurred next fell into the latter category. A roomful of otherwise ordinary people morphed into Navy Seal stalkers—as though the entire morning had been basic training and the afternoon was real combat. Jim and Stan escalated the stalk, working the room and navigating through the labyrinth of my multiple acts that had showed up without my permission—Fatal-Attraction Woman, Bossy Bitch, Seeking-Daddy's-Approval Girl—and, of course, the Ice Woman cameth, too!

Sunday afternoon we reconvened in the loft again at 1 PM sharp. As on the previous day, the chairs had once again been placed in a mystical round, this time as if surrounding the sacred Arthurian table, and the room had magically transformed from mere loft to athanor—the furnace, legend has it, that with a meticulous measure of heat and time, under the direction of the alchemist, is capable of transforming lead into gold.

A day and a half of stalking had thus far left no act unturned. The stories we'd all come with, sold ourselves on, had been skillfully exposed one by one, so that vulnerability, self-honesty, and self-respect were the transformed gold that remained.

"Surrender to the stabbing, for there shall be no wound," Jim said, his opening line slicing through the clarified air, an elixir of spent stories and new possibility, as all twenty of us settled in our seats, weary but enlivened by the bonds of authenticity we'd forged. "By participating and playing the game, you've each surrendered to a sword of discrimination that leaves no wound. Cutting away illusion, exposing the parts we play as distinct from our essential selves, we have hit at our core: basic goodness, nobility, and dignity." Then he went on to explain the closing process, which turned out to be something like stalking in reverse. With honesty and generosity, each participant was singled out and acknowledged for the remarkable character traits we had displayed throughout the weekend. As our acts and stories had been exposed, so now our traits such as generosity, compassion, humility, kindness, courage, nobility, dignity, humor and wisdom were also exposed, witnessed, and validated. Each "reverse stalk" was a bandage of compassion and a salve of human kindness that is rarely experienced except when tragedy strikes and our common humanity eclipses religious belief, status and color and comes to the collective aid of fellow men, women and children.

My life has convinced me that the key to any change is awareness . . . and acceptance. The mystic G.I Gurdjieff, in speaking to his own students, is quoted as saying: "Remember, you come here having already understood the necessity of struggling with yourself—only with yourself. Therefore, thank everyone who gives you the opportunity." What happened that weekend in The Event marked another truly enlightening choice point of my life. My gratitude for the process and everyone in that room was palpable. The prison doors of my stories had been unlocked, awareness had been ushered in, and the warden of genuine self-acceptance had walked me out that day.

Fast Forward. Two years and a dozen Events later, hearing Jim's "Find God and serve something greater than yourself" felt somewhat like a voyeuristic intrusion. How did he get this insider information about me? If I didn't know better, I'd have asked if he also liked what I'd done with my living room drapes. Jim had articulated a longing that I didn't know how to speak for myself; and even if I did, I was stumped with what *to do* about it. Tears pooled in my eyes from the oasis of my longing as the thought asserted itself in my mind: "You need a spiritual teacher. You can't do this alone!" It was a left-field thought, a bit like hearing myself say, "Go to Afghanistan and start a Women's Rights movement." But my next thought actually contained the seed of a real prayer. "Wait a minute," I paused to consider. "Jim has a guru. Maybe he can put in a good word for me."

FOUR

Enlightenment Schmitenment

Enlightenment is ego's ultimate disappointment.

CHÖGYAM TRUNGPA

*I*f you'd asked me back in 1995 what provoked me to leave my pedestrian life to go live off the land, mostly naked or in buckskin deer hides, I would have told you it was a good house-sitting gig. This would have been mostly not a lie. I would have fudged the part about the genetic vise-grip that compelled me to find myself—and God—the way Gollum was gripped by "my precious." My hyper-self-consciousness about the opinions of others would have selectively omitted the part about the smorgasbord of psychotherapy, Events and self-help books I'd consumed.

You see, despite the deeply transformative experiences of becoming a mother and mastering transcendental Events, I remained unconvinced that I was not fundamentally flawed—bereft of self-love and God—unlike the rest of humanity. People whom I knew *personally* seemed *whole*, or directed, as if by a clearly defined mission statement. Many were on a first-name basis with Jesus, Great Creator, Allah, or even the Buddha, while I was this close to concluding that I had been a heartless mercenary in a past life and that all of the gods, sons of gods, and demigods had collaborated to put a curse on me, casting me into a superficial hell to wander, dyslexic, without an identity or a soul.

Then, by some Houdini of fate, I stumbled, wouldn't ya know, into God's Garden in the summer of '95, where I would have my next, and this time positively seminal, enlightenment experience.

The Arizona monsoon season was overdue that summer, and the bone-dry earth and my pores were all gaping as wide as the mouths of baby birds in anticipation of rain's moisture. When I arrived at God's Garden in late June, it was a coin toss between which emotion I felt more of: dumbfounded or deliriously happy. The verdant oasis was situated thirty miles from civilization in the mineral-rich plateau of the Verde Valley, sequestered on a cottonwood and willow-lined slope of lower Oak Creek, which snakes a path from Sedona to Page Springs. My friends Sunny and Sundari had invited me to live with them for a self-sufficient summer at their homestead—a Robinson Crusoe "island" turned Shangri-La. Two months prior to my arrival, they had hoboed to the spot in their restored 1941 Chevy flatbed, now gypsy wagon, in search of tillable land and water. And, like ya' do, had squatted beneath the plentiful shade of the riparian cottonwoods and begun building a shelter and growing their own food. When the landowner happened on them gardening in their buckskins on his land, instead of aiming his shotgun and with steely Clint-Eastwood composure saying, "Get off my land, you damn hippies," he amicably agreed to a trade. They would be allowed to stay, grow their garden and finish their shelter in exchange for caretaking and providing protection from vagrants on the rest of his two-hundred-plus acre parcel.

By the time I arrived, Sunny and Sundari had replicated Middle Earth (*I double-dog swear it*). You know . . . the homeland of the Hobbits, Frodo and Samwise Gamgee? . . . *Lord of the Rings* trilogy? If I didn't know better, I'd have said that the location scout for those movies had evidently found Sunny and Sundari (much like the landowner) half-naked, tending their veggies in God's Garden, and said to herself, "You cannot make this shit up!"

God's Garden was the name my friends gave to their squatters' rights acquisition—a fusion of hippie-chic, master craftsmanship, and primitive technology. They had made a rammed-earth lodge in the side of a south-facing escarpment, complete with lodge-pole pine and red rock stone walls, all harvested from the land. There was a massive, hand-hewn four-poster pine bed centered beneath a skylight highlighting polished sandstone flooring and adjacent to a red stone fireplace finished with (you guessed it) an animal-skin rug that Sunny had personally skinned and tanned. There was a handmade stained-glass split door that swung open to face the garden. The roof of the lodge was carpeted in green vegetation. Vines of morning glories tumbled over the eaves, spiraling down lodge-pole beams in shocks of violet and fuchsia, trumpeting their brilliant, mystical, sun salutation each morning, then shape-shifting into robed devotees solemnly bowing each afternoon, as if performing *salat* in rhythm with the solar cycle. The garden itself was a hymn to nature's diversity and wisdom: melons, peas, radishes, cucumbers, carrots, squash and, of course, salad greens in several varieties. Floral bouquets of bachelor buttons, calendula, cosmos and asters braided through the garden in a spectacle of color, and a deer fence made of locally harvested wood in perfect matchstick pattern with a perfectly imperfect saw-toothed edge formed a protective border to their Garden of Eden.

God's Garden was the quintessential definition of an oasis in the desert—a place of Zen simplicity and fine workmanship, the sum of which communicated a language all its own that echoed from every meticulous seam and purposeful corner.

Sunny's full name was Sunny Baba. He was one part master craftsman, one part master back-to-the-lander, and one part self-proclaimed realized being. In his early fifties, Sunny possessed baby-blue eyes which, for lack of a better word but not for lack of my trying to find one, "sparkled." The whole of his face, I decided, gave his eyes this sparkle, and the lift of his wide-stretched smile formed his features into a billboard of kindness and contentment. Six-foot-fiveish and tan from stem to stern, with natural blond hair streaked by incoming gray, Sunny appeared a refugee from the Southern California beaches where I grew up and the career surfers I'd known. On closer examination, however, his tan was a weathered patina of earth tones that clung to his lank muscularity like a farmer's rather than a surfer's. He had lived his half-century working with the earth, creating alternative communities from California to Nepal. But, sparkly eyes and tan aside, it was the tattoos on his face that greeted you before any other features got their chance. Maori-inspired patterns outlined the hollows beneath his eyes, like owls' wings spanning the broad mounds of his weathered cheeks, and a small red dot between the beam of his brows shot out five black strokes, like the sun radiating from a third eye.

Despite my bohemian beach-girl upbringing, I'd never known anyone with tattoos. I'd never known anyone who wore buckskin loin cloths. I'd never lived off the land, and I'd never met a self-proclaimed "realized being," or a Baba. The Sunny Baba combination was exotic and unself-conscious and irresistible, the way I imagine being invited to live in the Australian bush with a tribe of pygmies would be.

Sundari was Sunny's match in every way, though she laid no claim to realization, his last name, or facial tattoos. She was equally exotic looking, possessing a set of cat-shaped eyes that I'd have shoved a woman out of line for had I been present when they were issued. Her aquamarine eyes emitted the radiance of the gemstone—a light that traced its source to a well-developed inner life and a keen discrimination that I soon came to know and admire. Sundari's eyes set all her other annoyingly beautiful features in place the way planets orbit the sun. An herbalist and a master gardener, she had built half of God's Garden, made the stained glass windows, and fashioned exquisite beadwork on buckskins that commanded hundreds of dollars apiece. Honestly, Sundari intimidated me, right up to the time we laughed so hard we both wet our loin cloths. Her playful, joyous sense of humor and love of laughter matched my own—thank God—or one of us may have taken our buck knife out and scalped the other while she slept.

∽

"Eggplant! Ugh! I hate eggplant," I said, as the three of us sat sewing buckskin and discussing the variety of seedlings in the greenhouse ready for planting. I attributed my fierce opposition to this uniquely beautiful veggie to its slimy texture and hastened to redeem my harsh position, assuring my hosts that I would still help plant the seedlings, but "just don't count on me to eat them."

"*Who* doesn't like eggplant?" Sunny said, without looking up from the moccasin he was stitching.

"I don't."

"Who is the 'I' that doesn't like eggplant?" he said.

"Moi!"

Sunny put down his sewing, raised his gaze to meet mine with a gentle tilt to his head, parted his lips enough to reveal a pinstripe of white, and without any trace of irritation said, "Who is *you*?"

It wasn't so much the eye contact that got me, though it had a probing unself-consciousness to it. No, it was the palpable absence of argument in him, replaced with an abiding presence that I can only describe as contentment.

"*Me*—last time I checked," I said, using sarcasm to conceal the edge of discomfort I now felt.

"Keep checking," he said. "Check again, and again. Observe who it is that likes and dislikes. Are you *that one*, or are you *the one who is witnessing* liking and disliking?" All the while, he held me in his steady, relaxed gaze.

"I don't know which 'one' dislikes the eggplant, but whenever 'we' eat it, 'we' all gag in unison!" I joked.

Sunny smiled more broadly, though not the full splendor of the smile that was his capacity. Undaunted, he continued, "If you observe closely, you may find you cannot locate the solid self to identify as this *you* that you call Kristen. You may find instead that there is no person, and nothing but pure consciousness itself." And, like a moonbeam cast across the surface of a motionless ocean, he directed the full splendor of his smile at me, radiating delight across the room. Then he chuckled to himself, the way I would have if I had farted in a crowded public library, and resumed his stitching. "But then, I'm nobody but a bozo on this bus," he concluded.

The language Sunny spoke was unusual, matching the unusual of the whole hippie-chic, deer-tanning, garden thingy. "Who is this 'I' you call you?" he asked me again as he drummed the tightness of a deer hide we'd strung up the day before to dry in the sun till it was taut as a drum's head. "There is no separation between you and God. You are not your personality; you are *prior to* personality, and you are *That* which you are seeking."

"I've heard you refer to 'realized beings.' Is this 'no separation' some kind of enlightenment?" I said.

"Realizing our true nature *is* enlightenment," Sunny went on to say. "Awakening to ourself as pure consciousness, no longer identified by the likes and dislikes of a personality, we realize our true nature, which is God consciousness."

He then talked about *satcitānanda*, a Sanskrit word that translates as "being-consciousness-bliss." As he spoke, Sunny pressed the razor edge of a handmade scraping tool against the brittle hair of a taut hide and, with the artistry and grace of a master, both hands cupping the tool in a downward diagonal motion, sliced through hair and the first layer of epidermis, removing the animal's once-animated coat. Matted clumps of brown, gray and downy-white fur drifted to the ground beneath our feet.

In the cool of the earth lodge during the heat of the afternoons we listened to tapes of Western spiritual teachers, gurus, on a battery-charged tape player found at the Salvation Army. On Sunday evenings the three of us would huddle in the cab of Sunny's circa-1960 Toyota truck and drive to town— to Sedona—where he held a *satsang*. Satsang was another Sanskrit term he taught me, translating it as "association with good company" and "a discourse with a teacher."

These Sunday evenings typically produced no more than three or four of Sedona's transient spiritual seekers with random questions about spiritual awakening and the nature of "enlightenment." On several Sundays no one showed, and the three of us would sit together in silence, meditating, or I would ask Sunny questions.

On one such Sunday evening on the cusp of August, the three of us sat quietly in the dedicated space of the Sedona Healing Center waiting for others to arrive. The summer heat hung heavily and the atmosphere was motionless, apart from a nomadic warm breeze that wandered almost imperceptibly through the open door at the back of the room. A large bronze statue of the Buddha with a wreath of crystals surrounding it and a small round table with a vase of flowers at its base dominated the center of the room behind Sunny. "Why do some people have a guru, or become students of these Western spiritual teachers we've been listening to, while others, like you, simply realize their true nature without a teacher?" I asked him.

"All paths that bring an end to the search and lead to the realizing of our true selves are valid," Sunny said.

"Such as?"

He proceeded to explain about four traditions—routes— spoken of in India, each a path to realizing union with God. The *jnana* path, he told me, uses the mind. Through study and attainment of knowledge one may be liberated and realize union with God-consciousness. The *karma* path is one of activity, right attitude and service to humanity, sacrificing self and thereby accumulating good merit to achieve liberation. The *raja* path is the control of the mind and body using meditation and yoga, among other rigorous practices. And then, I learned, there is the *bhakti* path, meaning devotion to a personal Beloved or guru. Through attention, devotion, and service to the guru, the devotee herself may be liberated into the very consciousness of the guru.

The question of a guru still pestered me. When I mysteriously landed in God's Garden I was already well into my search to find a god. I had lived in Sedona and been exposed to this mecca of spiritual options—from channeling, to sitting on vortex power spots, to sweating in Native American lodges. I'd even met one guru, Lee Lozowick, and read a bit from his books, but the issue wasn't handled for me. Through daily activities at God's Garden, listening to other gurus on tape, and the Sunday satsang with Sunny, the ideas of liberation from self-reference and God being not separate from my very self drifted on the winds of my awareness and fanned the smoldering embers of longing for the One I'd been seeking.

Without the use of illegal drugs, the synchromesh gears of my awareness glided quickly from first to fifth during that summer, and, without my conscious effort, liberated my bridled perceptions of self-reference into a heightened consciousness that animated everything I did and saw. "I" was dissolving. All I had previously defined myself as was merging into itself and into God's Garden at once.

Perhaps I fell into this slipstream of God consciousness by living free of power grids, indoor plumbing, and grocery shopping. Or it might simply have been the monastic solitude that slowed everything down, lubricated my spiritual gears, and catapulted me from Self Central into God Central, like the old TV character George Jetson in his zippy space car. As I think back on my time in God's Garden, I believe that no one thing was responsible for this opening to God. Rather, it was a "the whole is greater than the sum of its parts" type of conspiracy, ignited by the fuel of my longing to unlock the prison door of my consciousness.

It's possible that Sunny *was* a "realized being." I'm not sure. What I am sure of is that Sunny was a master of humble service to nature, of creating extraordinary beauty, and of joy and contentment living harmoniously with the earth. And, in his and Sundari's company in God's Garden, I located something my soul had been searching for—*God in me.* An illusive, divine nature appeared, no farther away than the soul keys I held in my hand even as I had cursed and frenetically searched for them. Discovering this *God in me* freed me from the prison of self-consciousness and the self-absorption that was all I'd known, and I fell swooning into the cave of my own heart, into a state of uninterrupted bliss.

∾

So, says lee,
you want God?
You want blisses?
What is it worth to you then?
Is it worth your health,
your peace of mind,
your equanimity?
Is it worth your sanity?

If you want to imagine God,
you may get away with it very
inexpensively—only act like
your mind is untroubled,
act like it's "all one" and suffering is an illusion.
But if you want to meet the Creature face
to Face, ah, sighs lee—
you must be prepared to be
misunderstood by your intimates,
ostracized by your friends,
shunned by the worldly.
Yet how ridiculous to even allude
to what you must be prepared
for—no preparation is the only preparation!
All of this babble. Is it poetry? No, it's
trash—throw it out—forget lee said
it—forget you read it.
Do you think you understand? Have you
swum on the moon? Have you watched
your own birth? Has the sun burnt
you to a well-roasted crisp?
Do you think you will be full of wisdom
if you realize God? You will be a
drunken fool, a pauper, a twisted man.
Of course you still say you want God.
Then have Him if you wish.
lee mourns you then, and celebrates you now.

—Lee Lozowick, *Death of a Dishonest Man*

Etched in the stone of the universe are immutable laws: like gravity; like every beginning has a middle and an end; like all human constructs can and will be deconstructed. And, as it turned out for me, enlightenment was not the sought-after trophy of the spiritual quest but the booby prize. Following my brief summer of enlightenment in God's Garden, I learned all too quickly that these laws will be enforced, like it or not! It was inevitable that I would return to "real life," to my real home with my real partner and real child, real bills and, well . . . I think you know where this is leading.

Once removed from God's peaceful no-assholes-and-no-commitments Garden, as effortlessly as I had fallen into that slipstream of bliss-consciousness and "my enlightenment," I fell out. The black rain of that fallout left a residual that was nothing short of a wriggling snake pit of multiplied "I's." Apparently, while I was blissed out, the "I" that didn't like eggplant had taken the liberty to spawn. I felt an existential crisis coming on and dragged myself to the mirror to get a good look at me (?) and all the other "I's" now teeming with opinion, irritation, objection, judgment, vanity, fear, likes and dislikes.

As difficult as it was to admit to myself, even in the privacy of my own home, what I saw staring back at me was "Consciousness Barbie" wearing handmade buckskin moccasins and matching buckskin handbag. My highly enlightened ego had apparently turned God consciousness, love and bliss into a *new* identity—a very special spiritual *someone* to add to the opinionated eggplant hater, the dyslexic, the mercenary soulless wanderer, and lo, the dreaded Ice Woman! The vortex of my mind was swirling with thoughts that, oddly enough, all revolved around me. Thoughts of what a horrible mother I was to have tiptoed off in the tulips of God's Garden. Thoughts that I'd probably have to move to a trailer park, feed my son Sam on Spam and Cheez Whiz sandwiches because no one would pay hundreds of dollars for my buckskin and beadwork the way they did for Sunny's and Sundari's! And, of course, there were the usual thoughts of whether or not I'd age as well as Madonna has, since she and I are only one year apart. And hey, as long as I *was* questioning this, I also speculated, golly gee, that if I did age as well as Madonna, maybe I would get a call from my old modeling agency that would offer me hundreds of dollars for my new Consciousness Barbie look and we wouldn't have to move to that trailer park and eat Spam and Cheez Whiz sandwiches after all.

Not long after I left God's Garden, Sunny and Sundari planned to move to California and study with one of the gurus we'd listened to on the Salvation Army tape recorder. On instinct, I knew Sundari and I might never see one another again, so I arranged to meet her for lunch at a local health food store. There, in the hustle and bustle of the afternoon lunch crowd, between bites of beet, beans and assorted greens, I lamented to Sundari, "I don't want to waste my life on the mundane personal dramas I once did, when love and pure bliss consciousness are my true nature. I should be spending my time in contentment and silence and . . ."

I hesitated, mid-sentence, to look up from my salad and make eye contact before I continued. Across from me, Sundari had placed her fork neatly on her plate, while her aquamarine eyes held me in a disarming glare that cut across the table, sending a message that required few words to convey. For all her kindness, she was a force to be reckoned with, and I suddenly felt heat flushing my cheeks and the same intimidation I had felt, months ago, just prior to peeing in our loin cloths.

With the skill of an aikido master, she wheeled into the gulf of my hesitation to redirect the conversation. "Don't cheapen what you experienced. Go deeper. You have to do your own work and find out for yourself what is and is not real. Bliss and Oneness are just experiences," she said, pausing just long enough to relax the vise grip of her gaze with her calming smile. "Enlightenment is nothing more than a concept without your personal investigation of *what is prior* to all experiences. Don't waste the opportunity or you will remain stuck in superficiality and empty understanding. Go deeper."

Leaning across the table, she tenderly placed her out-stretched hand on the back of mine. In that moment, I felt love rising from the deep well of her remarkable eyes into her touch, and the heat I received was more radiance than a reckoning, ushering from her substantial inner life.

We sat together, finishing our meal, while I burned with the guru-like nature of her presence and her words. What I realized in that moment, though it took me years to articulate it with any degree of clarity, was that "my enlightenment experience," as real and seminal as it was, was only superficial rain deposited on a subterranean reservoir of longing in me. To live an authentic, God-centered life, beyond experience or intellectualized notions—this was my truest longing. And right there, in Sundari's company, I knew with certitude, though I had no way of knowing how, that I was going to have to pay the price for it—a payment of devoted consistency to practice, and the other half of Jim's recommendation from three years prior: "Serve something greater than yourself."

As Sundari drove away, out of the parking lot of the health food store, I felt destitute and utterly alone. I arrived home feeling bankrupt and once again bereft—this time of hope—that the enlightenment seeds planted in God's Garden would ever germinate perennial value. Longing. Hopeless. My soul yearning like the mouth of a baby bird searching for sustenance.

FIVE

Meeting the Man

...when I first met You
I imagined You were the dispenser of Freedom.
Little did I know
that it was Slavery You were selling...
        —LEE LOZOWICK, *DEATH OF A DISHONEST MAN*

W hen I first met my teacher I was non-plussed. And disappointed. My first thought was "Huh?" My second was "Lose the turban."

I had been living in Sedona, Arizona, and attending a study group of his teachings—"he" being the Western spiritual teacher Lee Lozowick. Meeting "the man" who Jim (and some of the others I'd met through The Event) called "guru" was the first stop on my Find God Crusade.

I'd read a couple of Lee's books, as they were being used in the study group, but they may as well have been written in pig latin. I was not finding a connection to his words, so I tossed them aside for a while to collect dust on my bookshelf. Any resonance I felt with *him*, I felt through his students. It wasn't so much what they said or what they did—and lord knows it wasn't their renunciate fashion sense. It was something more basic, radical even. They (at least some of them) demonstrated an essential clarity, and an authenticity—as if they were conduits for a river of being and knowing that flowed from a reservoir of significance that I felt I lacked, yet longed for. I was after whatever *that* was, and the common denominator was the man they called their guru.

"The man" was white and from New Jersey. In his late forties, maybe fifty, I guessed. His salt-colored Joe Cocker hairdo and mustache-beard combo translated to me as Greek Orthodox priest more than guru. On the night I met him he'd chosen a plum-colored turban to accessorize a pair of black balloon-leg pants and Indian kurta shirt for the occasion. The turban sat lopsided on his head, giving the visual of a pell-mell-plopped beehive, which at any angle shouted "incorrect." I made a mental note to self: *Fashion challenges appear contagious. Could be game changer?*

Through force of will I shifted the turban to the background, the way you do with an optical illusion, which helped me to focus, more or less, on his words, but also shoved his eyes out into plain sight. Lee had silvery-blue kind eyes—glacial blue and a kindness that was unexpected in that it was devoid of affect and sentimentality. When he laughed, which he did a lot, his laughter rippled up the way air bubbles surface from water and bounced his chest in heaves. His turban-wrapped head would arch backward, his lower jaw would unhinge and expose his upper teeth—a perfect row of rectangular enamels.

Each time he did this, I couldn't help but think of those PEZ candy dispensers I used to spend my allowance money on when I was a kid; their Loony Tunes character heads atop a neck-like tube that was filled with rectangular, tart candies that popped out of the neck each time the head was tilted back. The effect of his laughter, I admit, was infectious, though on this occasion it had the unfortunate side effect of dismantling the ill-advised turban so that he spent the better part of the evening re-coiling and repositioning it. The whole of the visual collided with expectations of a guru the way a Hieronymus Bosch painting in his day was a collision of heresy, hallucination, symbolism and the expectations of art.

I confess, dear reader, that I had neglected to read *Gurus for Dummies* in advance. Likewise, I was as yet unfamiliar with the previously mentioned checklist from the Upanishads—the one that would have given me a few useful pointers to identify a true guru. Barring that help, I was left to my own devices, employing such criteria as:

- of East Indian descent?
- emanates a sense of holiness and nods with saintly magnanimity?
- has a proper-fitting turban?

On first impressions alone he would not have passed even *my* naïve measures, and was, truth be told, quite ordinary. All right—except for the turban. For starters, he was irreverent. I didn't expect that in a guru; but, for me, irreverence is endearing in, say . . . anybody. On this account alone I stuck it out.

Next, he was self-deprecating, like many of my favorite people are. So far so good for a stand-up comedian, or qualifying for a best friend. But for a guru? He was outright vocal in his derision of the New Age movement, equating it, as I recall, with "a good bowel movement," and accusing his audience of enlightenment-seeking and guru shopping. "You have plenty of self-proclaimed gurus here in Sedona. You can have your pick, or buy enlightenment on the corner. Why have you bothered to come here? You must think I'm an enlightened master?" he said to a room filled with fifty or more of the town's most ardent spiritual seekers. "I bet some of you even think Jim here is enlightened too, don't you?" Lee said, sober as church, while he re-coiled his turban.

As the night wore on, I had to consciously shift my focus from the glaciers of his eyes to his full berry-colored lips, hoping I'd capture a few single words that would equate to concepts I felt certain he was offering. No such luck! Instead, I found myself laughing as though I were stoned, but also feeling paranoid, as the un-stoned in the room were all looking at me mystified by what I found so funny. Everything felt distorted, the way a fun house mirror makes you look or a merry-go-round ride makes you feel. The net effect was part cold shower on my fantasy that I was hot on God's trail and part contact high.

Still, casting back to that first meeting with Lee has always reminded me of scenes from the movie *Michael* where John Travolta plays the famous archangel sent to Earth to help a woman named Dorothy find love. Dorothy, a bit like me, jaded by a bad marriage, has vowed never to fall in love again. In a country bar with her, Michael heads straight for the jukebox and punches up the rhythm-and-blues groove "Chain of Fools" by Aretha Franklin. As the song starts, Dorothy watches with amazement as Michael, dressed in a long dark trench coat and looking purely out of place in a cowboy bar, waves his arms high in the air, arches back and tilts his head skyward, as if saying, "This one is for you, God." As he spins himself around, the way a dervish dips and whirls, trance-like, two women join him on the dance floor, positioning themselves on either side, and follow his lead. Another woman surrenders to her urges, puts down her drink, pushes away from her man at the pool table and meets the others in their rapture. One by one, women from all corners of the bar slip from their seats, leaving their men, all entranced by the sensuality of Aretha Franklin's soulful groove and the irresistible mood that Michael, the angel, is conjuring. Men stare, slack-jawed, and women attest to smelling chocolate chip cookies. Later, as Dorothy and Michael leave, Dorothy stoically says, "I didn't smell anything," to which Michael says flatly, "Oh, that's because I put a block on you."

At the time I met Lee, I was unfamiliar with the story of the Ras Lila, the fabled dance of Lord Krishna that drew thousands of cowherd women to slip away into the night to enjoy ecstatic love play with him, the blue-skinned god. In hindsight, I realize that it was Lee's unconventional appearance and irreverent play that threw me off the scent in that first meeting, blocking me the way Michael claimed he blocked Dorothy; that is, until she was willing to see him for who he was, and let love in.

∽

My riff on an old maxim of the path:
When the student is ready, the teacher will not make it easy to find him (or her).

∽

A standard envelope arrived in the mail at my house; its looping, yet legible handwritten script in blue ink addressed it to me.

The return address identified the sender as Lee Lozowick—the same man I had all but written off two years earlier, in my disappointment, as an eccentric, albeit colorful, character. As I carried the envelope into the house together with a bag of groceries, I felt a surge of adrenal hormones in equal parts excitement and trepidation. Cautiously, I pried the letter open. Inside, handwritten in the same script and blue ink, was a message on the blank side of what appeared to be a random page from a spent manuscript. "You can find enlightenment anywhere—you don't need to be a student of mine for that!" his first sentence read. "IF you're interested in radical transformation, and if clarity and 'knowing God' is as important as you claim—read some of my books, attend the weekly study group in town, practice meditation and we'll see. —Lee."

Two weeks prior, I'd sent Lee a letter in which I had extolled my fidelity to "the Truth," adding my determination to "go deeper" than the enlightenment experiences I'd had in God's Garden. And, in a grand mal seizure of naiveté, I confessed my spiritual goal of becoming a "lover of God, like Rumi." Furthermore, as if I had not sufficiently established the orbit of my oblivion, I blasted off into the boundaryless space of the real question burning in me: "To fully realize my aim, be a lover of God and awaken, do I need a spiritual teacher like you?"

As far as spiritual determination goes, I was a steam train barreling down the tracks. Which is why, of course, I interpreted the first sentence of his letter as him being facetious—a trickster's ploy trying to scare me off or test my resolve. My resolve was fortified, however. I made a beeline for my bookshelf and dusted off one of his books that I'd pitched there. As if his letter had lifted the block on me, my nose picked up the scent of the trail to the deeper realization I was after. As I began to read, his words offered hints of intellectual satisfaction, elegance and structure, as if I had decanted a vintage wine and was now inhaling its heady aroma.

Hungry to know more about this guru, I called a good friend from The Event who had become Lee's student. In desperation, starved for spiritual food and companionship, I invited her to lunch.

"I feel more lost than ever now, Sharon," I said, as iced tea arrived and I dispensed with small talk. "I've had this experience of freedom—of being free from the endless searching and the attempts at rearranging my personality. But now that the *experience* has left, I feel worse. Old friends and I now have little in common, and I don't know who I can to talk to or what to do about this longing."

As Sharon sat patiently, I drilled her with a rapid fire of questions, beginning with:

Do I need a teacher?

How did you know you needed a teacher?

How did you know for sure Lee was your teacher?

What are the requirements to become his student?

Sharon listened with grace, then shoved a wedge in the open door of my next inhalation. "Take Lee up on his recommendation," she said. STOP. "Attend the local study group." STOP. "Begin meditation practice." STOP.

My eyes narrowed and my brows pinched together as I tried to mentally collect her instructions. "These practical steps will help you answer your questions," she said, reassuring me with a smile, like a mother nudging her child onto a school bus for the first time.

Sharon gave me the phone number of the woman who led the local study group based on Lee's teachings, and I wrote her info on the back of my lunch receipt. As Sharon and I said our good-byes at the curb, splitting off at right angles, I felt buoyed up, my steps now filled with possibility. The very next day I called Regina, reading off her number from the back of that receipt.

SIX

The Tavern of Ruin

> For those who have come to grow,
>   the whole world is a garden.
> For those who wish to remain in the dream,
>   the whole world is a stage.
> For those who have come to learn,
>   the whole world is a university.
> For those who have come to know god,
>   the whole world is a prayer mat.

>   —BAWA MUHAIYADDEEN;
>   TRANSLATION BY COLEMAN BARKS

*A*utumn 1996, in the high desert of Prescott, Arizona. The cottonwood and aspen leaves were turning copper and cranberry and the wind from balmy to crisp as I began my turning inward, away from seeking spiritual experiences and toward cultivating my inner life. As I write this, I am years into that inner practice, and I know less today than I thought I knew then about ideas such as "consciousness" or "reincarnation" or if our lives are one big collision course with destiny. I leave those mind-bending ideas to the pundits these days, though I won't deny that the passing of years has reinforced a hunch that our human incarnation is in collaboration with some great Divine conspiracy intent on bringing us into relationship with ourselves, *just as we are*—beauty-full, whole, with intrinsic dignity and joy.

Call it "following the heart," or "your soul," or the "will of God" . . . whatever! My own date with that Divine conspirator led me to an out-of-the-way, mysterious "tavern" (a concept that the Sufis honor) wherein other spiritual travelers, like me, were gathering to investigate the origins of this very conspiracy and awakening to their own true nature—their own deepest longing to know God.

In the offices of Athanor—the organization that conducted The Event and the name of the alchemist's furnace that turns lead into gold—we met every Wednesday night. The ordinary office space was transformed into a softly lit tavern, sans alcohol but with a mood that said hookah lounge or bordello. On the floor, in the middle of the room, a ring of burgundy meditation pillows was arranged. Against a north-facing wall, a knee-high table draped by a paisley-weave Indian silk shawl held a two-foot-tall marble stone carving of Hanuman, the monkey god of Hindu mythology. As the ardent devotee of the incomparable Lord Ram, Hanuman was on bended knee, poised, ready to serve God; his hands pressed together in *anjali mudra*, gaze fixed on his Beloved. A small votive candle burned before him, and a stick of incense dispersed contrails of a sweet fragrance: sandalwood, amber and frankincense. At Hanuman's foot, a gold-framed picture of Lee, also on bended knee before his own teacher, the venerable beggar-saint, Yogi Ramsuratkumar. Lee's hands were clasped in those of his Master and his gaze was fixed, as was Hanuman's, on his Beloved.

Regina and James, two long-term devotees of Lee, led the weekly gathering, beginning with a brief meditation practice, followed by study of the teacher's writing and poetry. The core group consisted of two regulars . . . and now me . . . with occasional visits by random students who lived at Lee's American ashram, or in town. A curiosity seeker would pass through, but rarely return. And there were times when a practitioner of another spiritual school would make a cameo appearance, sharing similarities from their own devotional practices or tradition, be it Sufism, mystical Christianity or Buddhism.

To attend the study group did not require a commitment to Lee or to his school, but rather a genuine dedication to personal inquiry (the willingness to dive into the assumptions of the mind), to clarified intention, and to practice. "Root out blind following" James and Regina both admonished, if once then a dozen times, adding, "This group is not intended to enroll new students."

Regina read a quote from Lee's book, *The Alchemy of Transformation:*

> A follower is somebody who likes the ideas connected to a spiritual school or a spiritual teacher, and is willing to do anything for the idea, but has no resonance in the body. Followers, therefore, are very dangerous people because they have no sense at all of the repercussions . . . They are like lemmings, willing to go off the cliff . . . they will die for the cause and thus have a strong

tendency to become fanatics . . . this indicates a very dangerous personal dynamic. (63)

"At the heart of this path is devotion," Regina said one Wednesday as the launching point for our discussion that evening. "In India this tradition is known as the *bhakti* path, the path of devotion. Our context for practice in this school is radical reliance on the guru."

Regina and James led us through a labyrinth of the school's teaching, which unveiled itself as a tapestry of traditional and esoteric paths: theistic Vaishnava Hinduism, non-theistic Vajrayana Buddhism, the mystical Baul tradition, along with a heavy influence of the mystic Gurdjieff's "Fourth Way," complete with its unique practices appropriately named "The Work." Eureka! I'd struck the pay dirt of spiritual traditions and gods—and no god—to study. It was, however, the begging minstrels of Bengal, the Bauls, singing and praising God and reminding me of my curious encounters with the Hare Krishnas of my childhood, who most captivated my attention.

The Bauls, an iconoclastic band of "mad," or "mad-for-God" men and women, sing and dance in ecstatic, mystical longing for their Beloved. Bound by no human's ideology or dogma, these "mad ones" defy social norms, live by begging, dress in clothing they patch together from rags, smoke ganja and are considered outcasts and contraries who have no regard for religious trappings or the caste systems. These spiritual renegades even drew the attention of Bob Dylan, who sang with them on his early recordings with The Band, as did other celebrity rock musicians. I could not help but notice the similarities of the Bauls to my take-away impressions of Christ and his disciples in their heyday:

1. Nomadic wanderers
2. Outcasts, hanging out with whores, drinking wine with the unwashed, and living off the generosity of others
3. Preaching a crazy, renegade message in parables and "tongues"
4. Deemed by "the church" and society as mad, heretics, and unorthodox

Though these Indian beggars were as foreign and weird to me as were those Hare Krishnas with their hand bags, I dug their renegade approach. Their views of God as the "man of the heart" paralleled the significance of Jesus—that radical whom I once found in my own heart. These God- and ganja-intoxicated nomads, free of moralistic and religious dogma, were connected to God in a way no definitions could constrain, and I felt kinship and a strange reunion. I felt Christ in the midst.

Lee readily identified his teaching with these iconoclastic minstrels, and spoke of his school as the Western Baul tradition, with an overarching context of "enlightened duality." This term referred to nondualism as ultimate Reality, with an emphasis on living in and through the dualistic nature of life—in the body, through the body, accepting *what is, as it is, here and now* (a phrase he borrowed from his much-admired friend, the French spiritual master Arnaud Desjardins). His was not a way of personal enlightenment for the sake of "my" freedom from "my" illusion, to relieve "my" suffering. Rather, it was an immersion into life to discover the One, the Beloved, the elusive "man of the heart" in the midst of ordinary life.

Wednesday nights became my addiction—to spend as much time as possible in study, in the company of these other students, in what was fast becoming my "Tavern of Ruin." I had heard about such a mysterious Sufi tavern where men and women talked in a twilight language, drunk on a wine poured from an unseen pitcher, merging with, awakening to, and ruined by Love.

∾

Pause. *Rewind.*

Did she say "radical reliance on the guru"? This did not sound anything like the iconoclastic Bauls—the love-struck, defiant, Dylan-befriending band of spiritual radicals. This sounded an alarm . . . as if someone had stormed into our God-intoxicated tavern yelling *Sieg biel*! I came to this oasis for liberation, not bondage to another man's dogma—some man with an ill-fitting turban whom I barely knew, despite his kind eyes and bad-ass humor. This "reliance" stuff was way off the reservation and smacked of born-again church all over again. This was the point at which I began saying to myself, "Put your hands up, and quietly step away from the vehicle."

Nonetheless, I stuck it out while repeating a new mantra: "Refuse blind following." Lee wasn't pushing anything on me, and in fact he kept me at arm's length, withholding invitations to spend time in his company or attend formal talks, despite my pressing the matter so I could get a closer look.

Three years passed while I wrote him letters, and he graciously responded without fail. "When can I come to a talk or come to *darshan*?" I'd asked, in one such letter, referring to the formal meeting of guru and devotee. He answered: "The strength of your practice is not dependent on seeing me. If you never saw me, you could still do your work. This is about you, not me. There will be time enough. Keep up the good work in study group.—Lee."

Undaunted, I wrote letter after letter, querying Lee on everything from the ridiculous to the sublime: challenges in my relationship, now that I was practicing with the guidance of a spiritual teacher; family matters; spiritual insights gained through my practice; work woes. You name it, I wrote to him about it, sparing no amount of the more-information-than-you-need-to-know detail. I also immersed myself in the spiritual literature he recommended—a wide swath of traditional classics such as *Spiritual Materialism* by Chögyam Trungpa Rinpoche, *Undiscovered Country* by Catherine Hulme, *In Quest of God* by Papa Ram Das, and *Rudi: 14 Years with My Teacher* by John Mann. Then there were Pema Chödrön, Tenzin Palmo, Suzuki Roshi, Kierkegaard, Vonnegut, Bubba Free John, Ken Wilbur, the poetry of Mirabai and Hafiz. And this was the short list. It was reading *Rudi: 14 Years with My Teacher* somewhere in the second half of that three-year study program that marked a watershed moment.

∼

I can't tell you, even now, *exactly* what it was about John Mann's book that created a turning point in my relationship with my teacher. Perhaps it was simple timing, or Mann's candid storytelling of his personal and complex relationship with his teacher Rudi—whose teaching style was so similar to what I'd experienced of Lee. Whatever the case, his book was like salt and pepper in proper measure putting the final touches into a perfect soup. His stories and insights were sprinkled into the soup of my study, my daily meditation, interactions with sangha (other students), and the pen-pal letters with the teacher I was coming to have a personal relationship with.

Reading John Mann's book—absorbing it, in fact—I knew, though unanswered questions remained and "radical reliance on the guru" was still way off-reservation, that I'd vow to take refuge in this guru, this dharma (teaching), and this sangha.

And the teacher, in time, recognized me as his student.

SEVEN

What's in a Name?

Do I exaggerate? Boy, do I, and I'd do it more if I
could get away with it.

—DAVID SEDARIS

*I*t is hard for me to believe that as I write this
it has been nineteen years since those early days as a student,
and even now the notion of "radical reliance on the guru"
continues to be a sticking point for me. Still, it is the most
possessed devotees—those mystics and provocateurs utterly
lost to their hearts' songs—who captivate my attention. Rumi,
Mirabai, Hafiz, Kabir and even Christ, the man himself, who
spoke in riddles about an unconventional reliance when he
said, "I am the Way, the Truth, and the Life; no one comes
to the Father except through me"—these radicals are my
spiritual heroes. What kind of wind fanned the embers of their
crazy declarations and their stories of union with the One?

What kind of love blew each of their minds, turning their once precious independence into a fool's aim and their reputation into empty meaning, compelling them, as Rumi said, not to "seek for love" but rather "seek to find all the barriers within yourself that you have built against it."

My first mistake was to read the book *Messages in Water*—that book about the Japanese researcher who tested hundreds of water samples that had specific words spoken over them or written on labels taped to them, along with music to serenade them; and who then froze each sample. His research findings spoke to my inner Louis Pasteur. Each of the samples of frozen water produced dramatic crystal formations: magnificent, glistening snowflake configurations when words like "Love," "Kindness," "Forgive me" and "Dalai Lama" were applied and music such as Beethoven or Bach was played, while ghastly, fourth-stage-melanoma-looking mutations formed when the water samples had labels like "I hate you," "You're stupid," or "Hitler" and when heavy-metal music was played. Compelling. Enough to beg the question, "What is in a name?"

Do the names we call ourselves have a unique vibrational or crystallizing effect in our bodies, the way the position of the moon and stars hold sway over tides and hormones or well-timed investment strategies, I wondered? I gave the questions what I felt was a good deal of rational thought, arguing that unwittingly sporting a name for the sentimental reasons that our parents may have had, or the married name we adopted due to cultural norms, pride or spousal good-doobieness, might be constellating crystals that looked like Swiss cheese, for all we knew. If a likeness of the Virgin Mary can form on a flour tortilla, for goodness' sake, who's to say my birth name wasn't forming a likeness of Medusa? Enough said. I determined to ask "the Man"—my guru—his opinion.

I was approaching seven years of study in the school, with four of those years being formally considered a student, joining the local sangha in events at the ashram: morning meditations, twice-weekly talks, and Sunday evening darshan with Lee. One fine spring morning in 2002, after morning meditation and a nourishing breakfast of oatmeal and green tea with my friendly ashram residents, I steeled my resolve about this name issue and approached the big guy at his desk in the office.

This was my second mistake.

I sauntered up to where he sat perfectly tranquil, ensconced in a book.

"Excuse me, Lee?"

"Yes?" He looked up, making direct eye contact—which, for better or worse, always gave me that naked-dream feeling.

"Given the recent and compelling research on water, how it crystallizes into brilliant or malignant forms when frozen, and the human body being ninety percent water and all," I said, "perhaps there is more to a name to be considered. What do you think of the importance of a name, and, more importantly, about my name and changing it?"

"Sure. Give me a couple weeks and I'll come up with something for you," he said.

"O-k-ay?" I stammered.

"Why not?" he said, with eerie cheer.

"Well, uh. No hurry. Take your time. I mean, I was curious about your thoughts," I said, having major second and third thoughts of my own. At that, he summarily stood, folded his book, dropped it to his desk in a deadfall from two feet, and smiled his tall, Cheshire Cat grin, graciously excused himself, then evaporated upstairs like Batman to his cave.

That appeared to be *that*.

The following morning, I emerged from the meditation-hall softened by candlelight and the aroma of Nag Champa, and moved purposeful as a monk as I took off my meditation shawl and collected my shoes. He (the big guy) slipped through the foyer door behind me and woke me from my transcendence with his distinct voice of gravel and gravitas, "Hey Kristen—here you go," shoving a slip of paper no bigger than a Zig Zag wrapper folded to the size of a postage stamp into my hands. "Here's your new name!" Startled, my eyeballs bulging like a chameleon's, I blinked and wondered to myself, *What happened to the two weeks part?*

"There's one stipulation," he said. "If you choose to change it, you have to change it legally."

Dumbfounded at the speed with which he had found something appropriate for me, I looked up from the beguiling paper resting in my now clammy palm. "Wa-wow. That, was . . . fast! Thanks," I said.

Staring back at me, with an upward jerk of his jaw, he indicated the paper. "Well, what are you waiting for? Open it!" I unfolded the note as he stood looking on and found written in his familiar handwriting (in miniature) the following words: "Name for Kristen: Tarini Bauliya." As I read the name in silence to myself I had a moment of flabbergast, then came to and forced my brain to signal my lips to purse and my vocal cords to vibrate, at which point I distinctly remember having what I now know to be a hot flash. The realization of what I had done dawned on me in that instant between flabbergast and paralyzed vocal cords. I had gone and invited my guru to change my name from my perfectly respectable and pronounceable name, Kristen Weaver, to a name with more vowels than is grammatically legal. As sound at last issued from my throat, I found my tongue had fallen asleep. I lisped, "Tar-eee-knee Bow-oo-lee-ya?," then questioned, "Am I pronouncing it right?" He nodded silently and grinned broadly, as if to say, "Sounds good enough to me."

"You've given me a new *first* and *last* name. Wow! I wasn't expecting that."

"Yep."

My mind was a lab rat in a cage strung out on meth, spinning frenetically to frame the picture of myself as "Tarini Bauliya" or view that unsightly mess of vowels on my business card. Then it hit me: *I'm not a lab rat or meth head*, though at that moment I wished I had a better explanation for the lapse in consciousness that had provoked me to give over such an indelible decision to my guru. I guess I was imagining something more elegant, like Grace Kelly—or, if exotic, one of those single-name names like Pink or Bono. I could have easily explained to the non-renunciate people I know, "I've always loved the name Grace, so what the heck," or argued that it was a branding strategy. I needed to call an emergency meeting with myself and fire the part of me that thought this was a good idea! The name was not at all what I had imagined, though clearly I hadn't worked out all the details. I am reasonably certain, however, that I would have chosen something that did not require a crash course in phonetics to decipher.

In desperation to make sense of his indiscriminate use of vowels, I asked, "Does it have a meaning?" to which Lee quipped, "That's for you to figure out. I'm not going to do the work for you."

WTF?!@#! was my thought while I watched Lee wheel around, his two-foot-long dreadlocks swaying cavalierly behind him as he moved to his desk. Nebbishy as Woody Allen, wringing my hands in existential angst before he got away, I shot back a pathetic volley of hopefulness over his disappearing shoulder, "Is there a nickname I can use?"

"No," he boomed emphatically and without so much as a backward glance. The finality of the moment was that of a positive pregnancy test. Mute, I held the holy sacrament of paper in my outstretched palm as my sangha mate, Kathy, who had been witness to the whole exchange, broke the tragic silence.

"May I have a look?" Her voice was a mix of reverence and shell-shock; with a nod she gestured toward the discreet slip of paper. As I shot her a wordless blessing, she plucked the note from my open palm and read the inscription to herself. "Lotsa vowels," she said, in her Boston-Italian accent. We both stood stupefied for what seemed like forever. What could be said? We both knew what I had done. And, as those smart asses "they" say, *What is done is done.*

As soon as I could form a thought, I framed Lee in my mind pulling down the Scrabble game the night before, plunging his hand into the letter bag, rummaging around and thinking to himself, "This oughta be fun," as he pulled out a fistful of letters and tossed them on the kitchen table. "Okay, whadda we got here? Oh crap, lots of I's. Well, it won't be the first time a student of mine had a lot of I's to manage—I'll make something out of this. Let's see, NIRIAT? Nah, that's no good. AIRTIN? Shit, I can't do that to her! Ah, I see—TAR, as in Tara. Oh, I think I've got something. Here we go, TARINI. Good, that'll suit her just fine. Okay, now for a last name. What can I make of the rest of this mess? AUIYABL? Vowel central again. IYALAUB, UBALIYA, hmm? Oh, wait a minute here, whadda ya know, there's BAUL right in the middle of this pile of vowels. You just can't make this shit up. That's it, BAULIYA. TARINI BAULIYA. Done."

∽

Things are never as they seem.

I assumed my new name on faith . . . Well, faith and seven years of kicking the tires on my guru's authenticity while wrestling with a payload of my projections onto him as savior and daddy, for starters. I'd come to his school for radical transformation, not for a savior to absolve me of sins I no longer believed in, or for a dad to replace the monstrous, slapdash father figures of my childhood. *Or had I?* Everything was up for questioning now at this point of changing my name, like:

1. What is the guru's role?
2. What is my role?
3. Now that it's official—I'm a student of a living guru— how do I avoid projections and suck the marrow from the relationship?
4. Where's the back door?

Questions like these were head banging against the walls of my mind. Add the fact of his ordinariness and personal quirks, and I was shoved deeper into the dilemma at every turn. Quirky habits, like insisting that his paper breakfast napkin (now used) be saved for him for the next meal. Question: *Conservation of the environment, idiosyncrasy, or cheap?*

Lee didn't personally use the Internet, or computers — ranting at times about the distraction of technology—how it was anesthetizing our culture further into blissful slumber. Question: *Valuable wisdom, opinion, or stodgy old school?*

When driving somewhere with him, he was always at the wheel, which inevitably threw my mind into mayhem. Think *Toad's Wild Ride.* Travel with him was not for the faint of heart. If you were prone to backseat driving, it was best to zip it, or pray to enter samadhi—quick! Question: *Was this a throwback from his youth and his confessed love affair with fast cars? Some esoteric teaching lesson? Or a straight-up need for an intervention to revoke his driver's license as an act of compassion for humanity?*

In a seminar he gave in France in January of 1999, he summarized the situation—the Work and the impossibility of effecting genuine transformation without it—this way:

> Ultimately this work is designed to throw every single one of us into a crisis so deep and profound, so mind-shattering, that we never recover. This is the realization that we come to: that as we are, as mechanical beings, freedom is a literal impossibility . . . There's only one way that freedom can be produced in us and that is to choose Work mind over neurotic mind. It has to be a conscious choice and the only way that we'll make a choice that's conscious is to see neurotic mind in its totality, in its death.

The Buddhists say of the Bodhisattva vow, the promise to work tirelessly life after life on behalf of all sentient beings: "Though impossible, I vow to do it." To which I've always said, *Really?* Though the vow is impossible, could one actually persist in the notion of possibility? And do I have what it takes to hold that the moment itself is the only domain of possibility? That the only way to reach the summit is through one conscious choice, one conscious step, one word or thought at one time? This sounded arduous. Tedious. Bor. . . ing! Yet, with every imperceptible effort to live aligned to this dharma, this jewel of human possibility, over and against the habituated or neurotic choices that my mind generally made up, the more impossible it would become to turn from the path.

I'd arrived at the feet of a genuine spiritual master. In my view, Lee was a most authentic human being; the kindest, most impeccably true-to-his-word man I'd ever met. He lived a life beyond his own personal preferences, refusing to allow those in his company to engage the slippery slope of premature enlightenment, and served this impossible vow, placing the liberation of all others . . . dare I say, *ultimate enlightenment* . . . before his own. And although I can feel his dry bones rattling in his tomb as I say so (he died in 2010), his methods fell into the crazy-wisdom category, putting him among the ranks of those other mad lovers enslaved to their Beloved whom I so admire.

In the same seminar in France, Lee went on to say:

Suffering is caused by grasping. If one grain of your suffering can be relieved here and now . . . then this seminar has been successful. If any one person can be moved one millimeter forward in their evolution— I'm not talking centimeter, but millimeter, forward— then we will have accomplished something. So all I'm interested in is what is possible in this moment, for any one of us, any two of us, all of us? What is possible here and now in this moment? That's all that interests me.

"Tarini Bauliya" did indeed throw me into a mental crisis. I dragged my feet (as if I'd had two left ones) to change my name legally, and winced at having to face the hundred-and-one questions from coworkers and business associates who would be justifiably curious. In the face of my own doubts about my lack of discrimination in blind following, I came to reason finally that it was just a name, not a kidney! And besides, I figured, you never knew when you were going to need an extra vowel. Or three.

Asked where my name comes from—"That's an interesting name." . . . "Is that your given name?" . . . "Does it have some special meaning?"—brings up all kinds of awkward. I have taken to saying, "Oh-uh, yeah, it's a long story. It's a Buddhist thing."

The average curiosity seeker is satisfied enough with that, since Buddhism has become broadly accepted in the West to the degree that I may as well have announced, "I'm a Democrat." Though not totally bullshit, since I *have* read Dzongsar Khyentse Rinpoche's book *What Makes You Not a Buddhist* and I am one-hundred percent down with his definition, my response is also not entirely true. I'm not "officially" Buddhist, just a cousin. Folks who ask me are well-meaning and all, but the truth is too much for most. Telling somebody that my name hails from an amalgamation of spiritual traditions—Hinduism, Buddhism, Bengali tantric *bhakti* madness—is weird, scary and a time management issue. Try saying that in passing to the perky hippie-chick at the health food store cash register. Then imagine the litany of questions that would follow, starting with, "Wow, sweet! So, how does that work?"

"Well," I'd quip, as I pecked my PIN number into the credit card machine, "it's basic Advaita Vedanta with a twist:

Enlightened Duality, rooted in a tradition of theistic guru yoga with an emphasis in non-theistic tantric Vajrayana Buddhism, expressed through art, music and theater, steeped in rock n' roll and the Delta blues."

"No kidding. *Cool.* So does your name have a meaning?" she might slip in just before directing me to "Go ahead and press the green ENTER button." At which point I would sigh heavily and with a hint of placating sarcasm say, "That's a darn good question. I'm still working that out!" I'd then stuff my groceries into my eco-bags and split before she asked another.

Tarini hails from the lineage of Kali, and finds her roots at the intersection of tribal Buddhism and Hinduism. She is almost always found near water—specifically the great Ganges or in the south of India, near Goa, where eleven rivers converge. A primitive tribal form of the deity is depicted with four arms holding elements of the charnel grounds (burning sites for the dead bodies), and seated or standing in a boat. This medieval Tarini was and still is revered by many as the protector goddess of those making their journey across the mighty Mother Ganges. Symbolically, she represents the mother-protector, both creative and destructive. She is said to carry souls across the turbulent waters of karma, a fierce protector as we make the uncertain transit through lifetimes to achieve a better birth in the next, or perhaps enlightenment in this one.

In the north, in Dakshineswar, India, along the banks of the purifying waters of the Ganges in Calcutta, Bhava Tarini is revered. She is the incarnation of the pitch-black Mother Kali, recognized by millions of devotees as the eternally compassionate, all-embracing mother-protector.

Whether in the south or north of India or in Tibet, Tarini and Mother Kali appear to be one and the same. Kali—the legendary bad-ass woman, skin shimmering blue-black as a moonless midnight, often depicted dancing on her husband Shiva's prostrate body or naked in ecstatic union with her lord, mounted on his erect phallus with a trident aimed at his head. She wears a necklace of freshly severed skulls and a skirt of amputated limbs. Her hair is typically matted or worn in dreadlocks, swaying in an unseen whirlwind of wild, holy madness; her teeth (fangs, actually) are bared to reveal a protruding blood-soaked tongue; a third eye bulges from her forehead.

Vanity Fair cover shot she is not. What she is, is the embodiment of uncompromising compassion, willing to sever heads to expose ultimate truth in any form; the Mother of all beings, she embraces all humanity—no aspect of the human experience rejected, no stone left unturned in helping us to know ourselves. And as the great sage Ramana Maharshi once said, "Your own self-realization is the greatest service you can render the world."

$$\sim$$

One Sunday morning in late June a year or so after I'd chosen to assume my new name, my new husband and I were basking in the afterglow of an ecstatic romp in the love sack. We were talking sweet afterglow language to one another, he saying my name and stroking my long, tangled locks, I stroking his sexy graying temples. As the glow wore off and we dressed for the day, the conversation turned to the mundane and he happened to make a comment that rang "religious" to my ear. So religious, and dogmatic, it made me question who he was and what he'd done with my husband. Without warning, a primal rage built in my big toe and surged up through my chakras, zero to sixty in a nanosecond. Mercury rising? Menopause? A woman possessed of an evil spirit? My head spun around, my matted hair whirling like the wild dreadlocks of Kali as I growled at him. I'm not sure, but I may even have stuck my tongue out at him. I was blinded by anger and stormed out of the room with the volcanic fury of Mt. Saint Helens! We were both lucky I didn't have my trident that day because I'm sure it would have been aimed at his head. My husband wrapped his arms around me in an act of compassion and began calling my name to bring me back from the abyss. "Tarini, Tarini, Tarini," he chanted.

My spiritual fantasy when I stepped into the path of my spiritual yearning was that scenes such as this would never happen again—that, through devotion and consistent spiritual practice, unflattering behaviors and my "lesser angles," as Abe Lincoln called them, would be transformed; and that I, like a genie from a bottle, would emerge in lotus position, mudras in hand, no longer a bull in a china closet, irredeemably vain, or the dreaded Ice Woman. Holy crap, was I wrong!

An adversary of spiritual window dressing, no matter how clever the facade, Lee championed my intrinsic dignity. He celebrated expressions of organic sincerity through my willingness to feel my own pain and authentic generosity, not by my becoming Miss Manners. He was the advocate for a teaching, a dharma, aimed at seeing reality in all its inexplicable grandeur and horror and for keeping my heart open to the latter as an antidote to spiritual fantasies, or to believing that a name makes me someone in particular, or special.

∽

It was not long after this event that I saw a CNN news report about a famous fashion photographer named Rankin who turned his camera on a few of the faces of the million or more people left homeless in the Congo due to the rebel wars that left as many millions slaughtered. The series was perhaps the most moving and graphic portrait of the grandeur and the horror of reality that this dharma teaching was urging me to meet without any façade, and with my heart open. Each remarkable face bore witness to the worst horrors of reality; to the murders of their children or parents, the rape and ransacking of lives and livelihoods. Their expressions were not facades of radiance but the indwelling grandeur of authentic human nobility: of having known unspeakable suffering, yet living triumphant with intrinsic dignity. Each image had a name inscribed on it that reminded me of those messages on water. Like my own name, each was a seeming jumble of too many vowels or a cluster of consonants, like Banza Mazamba, Kalimbiro Shambavu, Fursha Vumilla, and Karo Redi with the child she had named, ironically, Happiness. Above the photomontage was another inscription: *Cheka Kidogo*—the Swahili name for the collection, which translates, also ironically, as "Laugh a little."

EIGHT

Take the Job!

All of our days are numbered . . . We cannot afford
to be idle. To act on a bad idea is better than to
not act at all. Because the worth of the idea never
becomes apparent until you do it.

—NICK CAVE, *2,000 DAYS ON EARTH*

We don't know what we don't know until
we know what we didn't know.

What I didn't know when I set foot on the Western Baul
enlightened-duality path was that, despite three years of study
and courtship and the conviction that I'd found my way to
knowing God, I'd arrived with plenty of beginner's enthusiasm
and high intentions about "the path" but not much sense that
all of what I thought I knew would have to be examined on the
proving ground of personal investigation and experience.

Today, if I had any advice to offer you, should you be
considering stepping onto a similar spiritual path or engaging

work with a spiritual teacher, it would be this: Don't quit your day job! Although I could be accused of hyperbole at times (and a fair accusation it would be), this is not one of those times. I mean it. I've met plenty of well-adjusted, generous and compassionate people living contented lives who have never heard the word "bodhisattva," nor are they vaguely interested in unraveling the existential knot of existence or their own Buddha nature; yet, they still meet the daily rhythms, sublimities and heartbreaks of life with gracefulness, awe and dignity.

In my personal experience, this path, once engaged, is a no-turning-back thing—a lifelong process (or lifetimes, depending on who you ask) of shedding layers of your identifications with everything from dogs to gods; of discrimination and clarity that leads to the radiance and beauty at the heart of life, but not before you burn in the heat of practice and pass through your own squirming darkness, self-deception, and confrontation with the lies you didn't know you were telling and the shadows you were unaware you were casting. In short, this is not the path du jour!

Let's pause a moment and consider the artichoke—a daunting delicacy, I think we can agree, yet one with a veritable cult following, unlike the perfectly delicious ordinary potato, for instance. Perusing the succulent center of the awkward "choke," you encounter its thistles and barbs, but just one taste of its tender heart, drenched in butter, and you may be hooked, as I have been. So, too, with the determined spiritual aspirant. One encounter with Ultimate Reality and its bliss and, like an adventurous foodie, the intrepid seeker will either savor the liberating, unself-conscious moment and return to the path of practice with all its inherent obstacles, or chalk the transitory event up to an experience not worth the effort and instead order the French fries. And who would blame them?

Among my earliest naive assumptions about life on the spiritual path was the belief that serious practitioners—those singular candidates who summited—were mandated renunciates, lived on an ashram, and wore hand-me-downs. Such resolute souls were dispossessed, I thought, of all personal belongings, including their annoying personality quirks. They served in the guru's personal company and they were surely humble, obedient, and spoke Zen. This romantic notion was dragged out from the shadows to be seen for the malarkey it was the day my guru said, "Take the job." Three little words that proved to be an epitaph on the gravestone of my spiritual fantasy and that sealed the fate of my sadhana for years to come.

∿

I'd been offered a promotion at the company I loved working for—though the promotion met with my own mixed reviews now that I had found *The Path*. So I quizzed my guru about it: "Isn't this kind of professional upscale contraindicated by my spiritual aims?"

"Sounds like a good gig to me," he said. "Be sure you get what you're worth, and make as much money as you can and you will make everyone here green with envy!"

I registered his words, but wasn't sure I'd heard him correctly. So I countered to myself: *Serious students don't make big secular commitments or good money, from what I can tell. And whassup with the "green with envy" part? Aren't we supposed to be ridding ourselves of these pesty desires? What's his angle?*

Skeptical and waffling, I faxed a counter offer to him in France, where he was staying that summer, pressing him further—just shy of nagging—and raising my new and improved concerns. An envelope arrived in my mailbox two weeks later with the return address identifying the source, stamped PAR AVION. Inside was a greeting card covered on the front with Persian calligraphy. Instead of opening it at once to read my teacher's response, on the hunch that there was a hidden meaning behind his choice of greeting, I flipped the card over and found what I was looking for—the translation, like a secret decoder ring in the Cracker Jacks box. The inscription read: "When you reach the heart of life, you will find beauty in everything!"

Interesting, hmm. And your point is? I said to myself. Then I opened the card to find my teacher's message inside:

TAKE THE JOB!

These three simple words were written in all caps and underlined, large enough to fill both sides of the card, to jump out like a jack-in-the-box, and to startle the bejeezus out of me. Along the straight edge of the bottom of the card he wrote—in normal-sized letters—"You are doing what you do (in other areas of your life)—is *that* clear? —lee."

The guru-devotee relationship is a perilous one. Immediate are the projections and expectations and hopes we place on the guru, all of which must be navigated before we have a chance of piercing any gobstopping illusions. The jewel of the dharma, and the gifts of a genuine guru, are ever luminous and eternal. Yet to recognize and realize these gifts we must first pass through our own shadow, the pathology inherent in the relationship, and the pitfalls of group mind to get to the heart of life on the devotional path.

The student has free will. If she seeks counsel from her spiritual master in the domain of the mundane as she attempts to align with the *ultimate* aim of the program—as in any master-level apprenticeship—she must freely evaluate the input, apply common sense, and, ultimately, make up her own mind. Or, she might exercise another intelligent alternative, such as to keep on truckin' with her practice and avoid wasting the master's time on the mundane affairs that she can and should figure out for herself. After all, the guru's role is not career, marriage or sex counselor.

"My recommendations to you are just that, recommendations. And they are straightforward; you don't need to figure them out. They are at face value; no hidden meanings." My guru said this to me once after a series of cross-checking inquiries about his communications with me. I may not be the only Lucy Ricardo of spiritual students, but I'm certainly one of them—guileless and slow to get that the joke's on me. But I'm enthusiastic, and able to channel that enthusiasm to make work fun. And, for better or worse, I possess an indomitable drive to achieve my aims, whatever they may be.

I took the job sixteen years ago now, on my teacher's nod. Hold on . . . not really a *nod*; actually more of a head-butt. And that head-butt led me directly into the heart of life, the experiential proving ground my spiritual well-being required, where beauty can be ultimately seen in everything. I'd be lying, though, if I said that I can altogether see the beauty in my own shadows, yet.

∽

"I feel like I'm failing at this, Herb," I said to my boss, two years into the promotion. My boss was a six-foot-something rock-star sales guru of the crazy-wisdom genre, a swaggering paradox of capitalism and transcendentalism. At times, I would have bet good money he had been hired to sing harmony to my spiritual teacher's lead vocals.

"Failing how?" he said, the length of him outstretched toward the San Diego sunshine, head cocked skyward and eyes concealed behind his Annie Hall shades as he picked remnants of lunch from his teeth with a toothpick.

"I feel like I'm a fake and haven't earned the respect of my team. I'm doing everything technically right; we're hitting sales goals, but I feel there is something I lack. Maybe it was a mistake to move me to management—not everyone good at sales makes a great sales leader, you know," I said, fishing for his sagacious feedback.

"Tarini, the karmic wheel landed on you. Suck it up. Arjuna whined about the job he had to do, too, remember . . . in the *Bhagavad Gita*? Re-*freekin'*-lax—this is your dharma. You do your job and, trust me, they'll respect you." He then lowered his shades to reveal the espresso beans of his eyes flickering with roguish approval, squinted to form cinched curtains at the corners of his face, and arched his brows as if to say, "Is that clear?" Discarding the toothpick to his plate of lunch scraps with the disdain of Arjuna discarding a bloodied sword onto the body-strewn battlefield, he sprang off his chair and with a Pied Piper gesture waved me up and out of my self-doubt, back to our meeting, and back to do my job.

∽

Unlike the negative connotations of the word *guru*, the word *dharma* (as Herb had thrown it in my direction) seems to be enjoying a far more positive inclusion in our Western wordbook. The venerable Dalai Lama is respected by a global community for his unifying dharma of peace, kindness and forbearance; business gurus like Deepak Chopra have introduced the consideration of the dharma into boardrooms; and yoga instructors the world over are now spreading the good news about the dharma on, and off, their yoga mats.

In the Buddhist lexicon, *dharma* possesses the most comprehensive meaning of any word. *Dham* at its base is Sanskrit, referring to an action to reduce misery and unnecessary suffering. The verbs "to support" or "to protect" apply here as well. At this entry level then, we could say that the dharma is action that supports a steadfast understanding of natural laws in order to reduce misery and unnecessary suffering. This was what I wanted: to bring the dharma off my meditation pillow and into my everyday life. With my guru's head-butt and reinforcements from Herb, I moved ahead into the job with heartfelt intention to support the dharma through a life of action.

And, like Arjuna, I was to enter a battleground that I never imagined.

∽

A spiritual road warrior armed with practice and my "sales manager" shield, I hit the road. *What doesn't kill you makes you stronger!* I could almost hear my stepfather channeling these words through Gin-Breath Guy, who chatted me up as he metabolized his happy-hour drinks on a six-hour flight. I sat gracious and Buddha-like in the middle seat next to him, and threw up a little in my mouth more times than I can count.

All the world is God's playground. I retrofitted a hundred hotel rooms into places of refuge with a picture of my guru, candle, incense, and three miniature bronze deities: Ganesh to clear obstructions; Hanuman to remind me of great devotion and to keep my heart open, come what may; and the three monkeys—a primitive bronze of three tiny primates seated in a row, like devotees in seated meditation. These little guys affectionately reminded me of my whack-a-do monkey mind, of the practice of holding my seat (a phrase I learned from the contemporary and pragmatic Buddhist teacher Pema Chödrön), and of the necessity for maintaining my sense of humor (because few things are funnier than monkeys . . . doing anything). Flowers were surreptitiously cut from floral arrangements in hotel lobbies and rearranged on my travel shrines from San Diego to Seattle, Kona to Kansas City, Milwaukee to Montreal, and a whole bunch of cities in between. My version of God's playground included crowded shuttle buses, missed flights, lost luggage, hiring and firing, building sales teams, forging business relationships, designing sales strategies, hitting and missing sales goals, building a BRAND and more beautiful friendships than I can count, while some broke (but did not kill me) when they did not endure the valley of our shadows, and the test of time.

In the *Bhagavad Gita*, that mythic and epic tale of Lord Krishna and Arjuna alluded to earlier, Krishna tells Arjuna, "It is better to carry out one's own dharma imperfectly than to carry out the dharma of another perfectly. Nothing is ever lost in following one's own dharma. Competition in another's dharma breeds fear and insecurity." The karmic wheel had been spun for me. The dharmic dice had landed. My guru had kicked my bliss-ninny ass off the renunciate pillow and out into the real world, far from the beauty of his physical company and the illusion that it was necessary, just as Krishna kicked Arjuna's ass onto the battlefield to conquer the ultimate illusions: right and wrong, good and bad, sacred and secular, friend and foe, dark and light, life and death. Thanks to my spiritual master and that crazy-wise sales savant, my boss, together in some cosmic collaboration, I was forced to look honestly at myself and laugh at what I saw for the fourteen years that I worked this job. There, on the battlefield of real life, my dharma was revealed and my being was established in the doing.

∾

Still, self-doubt cropped up in every aspect of my life—in my relationships and in my spiritual practice; but perhaps nowhere more glaringly than in my job, in my work with others. This doubting voice was, and still is, with me, convincing me that I'm not good enough, that I'm not worthy, that I'm unloved; at which point pride often steps in to overcompensate for the imagined inadequacy. It's like I have my own personal AM Talk Radio show, dishing out commentary on everything I do, have done, attempt to do, say, or have said. It's jabbering away right now—big time—as I write these words. It's always set to assert low-grade opinions like, "You can't write, you're dyslexic . . . and left-handed. Hellooo?" Or, "Your audience for this book is going to be limited to your family, and even they may not read this schlock." Or, "This is a big waste of time, and a money pit!" Even years after admitting my doubts to Herb, my boss, grappling with the challenge of success at every turn, the voices are still transmitting loud and clear.

"I feel like I'm faking it," I said to my friend and coworker Disa over lunch one day a number of years ago. She and I had each accepted another promotion after a collective twenty-one years of successes at the same company. We were to start up a Canadian sales division without previous related experience and despite not speaking French as a second language.

"You and I suffer from Impostor Syndrome," she said. Disa was the Ethel to my Lucy, the yin to my yang, the peas to my carrots. Which is to say, we could finish one another's sentences. But on this occasion I needed more information.

"Most women feel this way," she continued. "Like we're faking it. Like someone is going to finally catch up with us, tap us on the shoulder, and call us out on everything we've ever accomplished, accusing us of being impostors." She picked at her wild-salmon salad.

"You mean like we're posers? I've felt that way my whole life," I admitted. "Everything I've ever done—from being a mother, to buck-skinning deer hides to near perfection, to leading sales teams these fourteen years."

Disa went on: "Women feel like impostors because it's a cultural expectation that men accomplish the big things; so when we women take the lead and do the accomplishing, we feel somehow that we didn't earn it—that we're faking."

"Huh—funny. So, we're *all* impostors when you think about it, aren't we?" I said, casting my glance across her shoulder and through the window of the restaurant to the spectacle of a snow-capped glacier towering above the Vancouver harbor.

"Yeah, I s'pose—but s'plain?" she said, channeling Ethel.

"What I mean is, we spend our lives building healthy egos necessary to gain skill and expertise, and we manufacture a persona to fit the roles—the CEOs, the environmentalists, sales managers, tech geeks, yoga teachers, presidents, whatever. But none of these roles are who any of us *really are*. I've become so identified with 'the role,' I've forgotten that my original aim was to serve God, do my work in the world, gain expertise . . . but not take *myself* or the *persona* seriously. I missed the mark, Disa."

"We both have," she said soberly.

Fortunately, years of practice have helped me to change the channel of my inner self-doubt to a more merciful channel—to my inner Lucy Ricardo who says Yes to life, gets messy doing it, and doesn't seek Ricky's and sometimes even Ethel's approval. I've also come to appreciate that the path is never a straight route to an endpoint. All paths bend and curve, and sometimes they take us in circles. This has certainly been true for me. All of these twists and turns, dead ends and rest stops *were* (and still *are*) the path. If, as the greeting on Lee's card to me said, "When you reach the heart of life, you will find beauty in everything," then it is this very traverse from great insights to illusion, ecstasy and then agony, joy followed by sorrow, love and then betrayal, trust and mistrust, openness and withdrawal, and so on, that allows us to know the truth of this lovely aphorism for ourselves.

Don't quote me on this, but I believe it was Pierre Teilhard de Chardin—or was it E.J Gold?—who said, "We are spiritual beings having a human experience." One of the spiritual greats said this, apparently, and it has helped me to make sense of my compelling impulse to know God and my stumbling into the company of this mad Baul guru. His first recommendation for me was to "take the job," knowing that I would take the dharma with me and meet my shadow—the very thing I needed if I was ever to live an unscripted, authentic spiritual experience in all my humanity.

Perhaps it is this simple: Perhaps the true guru is a spiritual friend who is also having a human experience, but one who did not forget who he or she *was* and why they came here. Perhaps such a spiritual friend is able to radiate beauty in everything, and so seekers like me are drawn to that radiance, as it serves to protect the jewel of the dharma by its full humanness. In my own case, it seems that the true guru has whispered, or yelled, past the white noise of my Talk Radio—urging me to *"Remember!* REMEMBER who you are: You are pure radiance, an illuminating human beauty, dignified and noble. Stop diminishing your brilliance by pretending to be a *somebody*, a sales manager."

NINE

My Mother's Daughter

Knowing nothing shuts the iron gates;
the new love opens them.
The sound of the gates opening wakes
the beautiful woman asleep.
Kabir says: Fantastic!
Don't let a chance like this go by!

—KABIR, VERSION BY ROBERT BLY

*I*t wasn't that long ago that I would have sworn the chances of my attending my mother's funeral were as unlikely as my attending a gun convention. Recalling the contempt I once had for her summons a wave of sorrow, now that my mother and I have crossed those turbulent waters to the transformative shores of remorse. Time and forgiveness have tenderly healed the wounds of our past.

The transformation from contempt to forgiveness was so radical, in fact, that it's hard now to remember what first got my thong in a wad. I'm not saying my mother and I are best friends today—that's corny. Or that she's my heroine—that's a stretch. Nevertheless, be it good merit in the Buddhist sense, reversal of karma in the Hare Krishna sense, or a walk-on-water miracle in the Jesus sense, I now genuinely appreciate time in my mother's company. We share the kind of deep love that is born of digging out of the trenches together, to emerge alive. Redeemed. The relationship we now enjoy is not based on concepts of what a mother or a daughter should be, but on who we each are, as we are: two people with all our blemishes and bruises.

While I haven't done a randomized, placebo-controlled study or anything, I have made an anecdotal survey of my women friends to find that "enjoyment of a mother's company" places me among a freakish, statistically insignificant minority. To the question, "How close are you?" responses range from the obligatory phone calls twice a year (birthdays and Christmas), to positively remote. "Remote" being that they thankfully live several states away from Mom, with a preference for continents.

Sometimes, our mothers (and fathers) die leaving estates, or sums of money in trust funds. I even have a friend whose dad left him a sizable inheritance in a tin can in his backyard. More often than not, though, we are left with regrets, unsaids, or saids we wish we could unsay, rewind, or redo. Had it not been for the uncompromising influence of my spiritual master, I am persuaded that I was destined to write my mother off and go to the grave justifying my story as to why.

Never mind enlightenment or realization—those things have absolutely no meaning in the real world

. . . If you could see God right now, if you can catch a glimpse of Reality, a moment of ecstasy, a laughing fit—that's something! If you haven't told your mother you love her in five years and you call her up next weekend and tell her that you love her, then that's it. I'm happy. I've done my job.

—Lee Lozowick, France 2001

My mother is a Gemini with good genes. At every age she has been a head-turner, and at seventy-six she is no different, drawing attention from men her age both ambulatory and driving motorized scooters.

"Hey, Mom, that man over there is looking at you and he's not in bad shape for his age, either," I say, elbowing her in the ribs as we cross the grocery store parking lot.

"Who, that guy doddering in his walker?" she says, as we hook arms, leaning in like two gossipy teenagers.

"No, Einstein, that one over there loading his groceries with the 'Obama 2012' sticker on his tail gate!"

"Oh great, honey. He's an old fart, probably living on Social Security, and he's probably still brainwashed by Obama's 'change' BS!"

"Well, it's a start, Mom. He's got motor skills, is in good shape, and at least we know he's left of center."

Like every woman my mother's age, she has her fair share of creases and folds in all the usual places. Sun-weathered and etched by a number of epic losses, she wears all of them well. All her teeth are rooted in place, filling out an angular jaw and her not infrequent gummy smile that resembles my own. She's fit and weathered as a rancher's wife, without the rancher, and her feet are often inappropriately shod—in wedgie flip-flops—for such a rugged soul herding free-range adopted dogs around her one-acre farm. She has four dogs. Excuse me, make that three—one died recently, so let the record show: three dogs, one cat, and ten laying hens, with the occasional wild chicken.

"Mom, there's two chickens roosting in the tree outside."

"Oh, those are the Flying Wallendas. They're wild chickens, actually. They don't get along with the girls in the hen house so they roost in the trees all night and range during the day."

"Wild? Are we talking migratory?" I asked, curious and only sort of kidding.

"No, you ninny, I bought 'em. They don't lay eggs and nobody wants chickens that don't lay eggs—so I took them. You know how I love the wild things!"

While not a bona fide eccentric, my mother is on the cusp.

I owe my mom a debt of gratitude for many things, but teaching me about the rules of life stands out most. In particular, the varied ways one can *break* them . . . starting with attending school. My mother was the first to excuse me if there was something more interesting going on, such as playing hooky, with her! I credit my mom, mostly, for my attitude toward reading instructions or the manual. I don't. Traffic laws, or waiting in lines at the grocery checkout—all merely guidelines, according to my mom. "Sheep! We're sheep and they expect us to continue to blindly follow all their rules while they fleece us blind!" Why, just this year, as we headed out to Trader Joe's to pick up groceries, she tossed on her ball cap, snugged it down over her chiffon of downy-white hair, collected her keys and reached for her beer.

"Mom, that's an open container. You're not planning on taking that with us, are you?" I said, three parts rhetorical, one part parental.

"Oh, puff," she shrugged, sweeping the beer off the counter in defiance. "It's just one beer." Think Huckleberry Finn and Mother Teresa. Oh, who am I kidding? She's a Gemini. Add a pinch of Martha Stewart, a cup of Dave Barry, and a nosh of Jewish mother.

Did I just mention my mother and Mother Teresa together, in the same sentence? Never. Still, some striking similarities have emerged with age, like the fact that she's made a second profession out of eldercare for ex-husbands and dogs, and she is bullish on compassion for the downtrodden. As for the rest, my mother could run an empire if she were so inclined; she has a wacky and dark sense of humor, and she can smell a good deal or a deadbeat from any distance.

～

My spiritual master once defined intimacy along these lines: delighting in the company of others as they are, in truth. Not only delighting in them when they agree with us and laugh at our jokes, but when their idiosyncrasies and annoying differences are accepted as the whole of who they are.

My teacher's definition would not exactly have described my relationship with my mom when my grandmother died. The script around that event would make for a Coen brothers black comedy. Though as grandmother's estate was being settled, no one was laughing. Instead, our lives were chock-full of double-crossing larceny and incestuous betrayal, the only thing missing from the picture being a wood chipper and a meat locker full of body parts. Money. Greed. Power. And, you guessed it, a full-fledged family feud. In an unimaginable, treasonable act, my sister and I, fed up with the double-talk about my dead grandma's wishes for her grandchildren's inheritance, determined that the only thing to do was to hire a New Age lawyer with a bad '80s perm and file suit . . . against our mother!

Sam was going on six. I was a single mom and afraid. Afraid to be a mom. Afraid my genes were a mutt and not a pedigree of moral authority or instinctual nurture. And my relationship with my mother? Well, I was tugging to become my own woman, crafted from parts *I'd* identified, not one dressed up in my mom's hand-me-downs. Where my mother saw a grocery line filled with sheep, I saw moments of quiet pause—a bit of order for a scared little girl caught in the crossfire of a chaotic and disordered childhood. Where she saw a brainwashed old fart, I saw companionship. I wanted to know where *I* began and where *she* ended. I wanted sovereignty and a clear sense of self . . . and I was in a mad rush to get it.

I can't speak for my mother, although, if I were to guess, she too was tugging at her cover, trying to show me, and herself, the ordinary woman under the MOM badge and the *I-Am-Woman* bravado. I believe she wanted to sever the umbilical cord that was wrapped around both our necks, depriving us of authenticity and acceptance and individuation. We were the Witches of Eastwick, whipping up a brew that would determine who was more powerful, or the "fairest of them all." All in all, a perfectly wicked storm raged for two long years, battering the windows and walls and nearly washing away the shelter of our relationship.

"Litigation, for example, is becoming an epidemic, indicative of a systemic violence in the world, the absence of dignity and a debt to the soul—individually and collectively—that we cannot afford to underestimate." Matthew Fox, the well-known author and theologian, said this during a talk hosted by our local college. I was there, and, no surprise, so was Lee. Dr. Fox spoke with a notable absence of negative judgment, yet his words were filled with passion about the crisis of our times, the loss of the sacred in our daily lives, and the pervasiveness of technology distancing human beings from the natural world. When his lecture took this curious turn to litigation, the moment was a Stephen-King-spooky one for me. I froze. Motionless as a snake digesting an oversized rodent, I could do little else but absorb the poignancy of Fox's indictment as my get-what's-mine lawsuit raged on, and the underestimated debt to my soul mounted.

When the program ended and folks drifted up the aisles of the auditorium, Lee angled stealthily through the crowd to sidle up beside me as I made my way to the front doors. "If you did not get the answer to your questions tonight—about the lawsuit with your mother—you never will!" he said. The meter of his speech struck two distinct downbeats—on *never*, and *will*. Then, dispensing with the diluting chitchat, the conversation was truncated as he zigzagged a path to the exit, and I watched as he disappeared into the moonless night.

◦◦◦

Nearly a year later, when a letter arrived addressed with my mother's familiar handwriting, we were already two years into our litigious, soul-sapping battle. I had had a full twelve months to digest Dr. Fox's message and Lee's communication to me on that night, and a year of relationship with my mother going to seed. The paradox of it? I was apprenticing in a spiritual school in which kindness, generosity, dignity and nobility were the tacit expressions of its aim. The crux of the paradox, for me, was pride. Pride, which after many years of self-observation I've come to identify as my "chief feature," as G. I. Gurdjieff coined it. *Chief feature* is that core psychological sticking point: the central knot around which all other neurotic behaviors affix themselves. Pride, I am not proud to say, assisted by a "stubborn will to win," is what stood between me and "getting it," as my teacher said, and it's what let my mother's letter grow mold on the counter for roughly a week. As it cultured there, it nagged at my innate curiosity and finally got the better of me. I opened the letter with my guard dogs tethered, straining against their choke chains. To my shock, however, it sounded and read like a combination peace treaty and love letter, steeped in the longing of a mother two years at war with the two people in the world she loved most, whose companionship and respect she ached for.

I don't recall the exact words she wrote, but the pain and sorrow were unmistakable. In an act of love and courage, she offered to lay down *her* sword—all opinions of who was right and who was wrong—in trade for *our* swords. My mother was the first to throw up the white flag, and she was not the "spiritual student." Ouch! That left a mark. She was offering to bring an end to the war by giving us the money we so righteously felt was ours, no strings attached, only that we come visit her at her home on Orcas Island in the Puget Sound of Washington.

My heart had been softening all that year as I studied and practiced, even though I did it with my heels dug in. As I read my mother's words, I could not help imagining what it would be like to suffer the loss of love and respect from my own son. The letter, though she had no way of knowing it, was an invitation that called to me, with perfect timing, to go deeper than the appearances of practice, to a level I had not been willing or able to access prior to that moment. If I was ever to cultivate genuine compassion, I knew right then and there that it would only happen when I was able to feel intimately what another felt and, from having experienced something of another's pain, join with them in their humanity. I held the letter and wept.

I had never asked my teacher a what-should-I-do question, but on this occasion I wrote for his recommendation. "Would you advise going to Washington to see her, or just dropping the law suit and letting time heal wounds? I'm sick about the heartache this has caused; sick that my son, Sam, will not know his grandma at this rate."

A note from Lee came back so quickly I had to check for pigeon feathers. With his characteristic frugality, he returned the same note I'd written him, but added at the bottom: "Duh! Go to see her —Jai Guru, Lee."

I called my mother the next day, thanked her for the invitation, and said, "Yes," I would come, "and I'd like to bring Sam."

"Oh, wonderful. That would be wonderful," she said.

Socrates declared that the unexamined life is not worth living. The saying, for whatever reason, has always made me think of the great devotional traditions: Muslim, Hindu, or Christian, with its contemplative monks and nuns. Several times a day, dedicated practitioners in each of these traditions will stop what they are doing and drop to their knees in observance, or prostrate themselves fully in prayer. Acts of devotion, yes, though more often than not, I imagine, they are expressions of a conscious choice to live "as if." A reflective, inner spiraling; an examination of the sacred against a backdrop of all the busyness and doing. As heads intentionally dip beneath the throne of the heart, surrendering to the true monarch of our lives— that great numinosity and mystery—we bow, suspending for those few minutes our small-minded concerns and habits of the unexamined life.

I bent over and bowed through the portal door of the six-seater puddle jumper, emerging into a sun-spackled Pacific Northwest summer day, as the props powered down and the engine hummed to a stop. Stepping down the unfolded length of the airplane stairs, I saw my mother waiting on the makeshift tarmac in an open field on Orcas Island. Sam emerged from behind me with a meteor shower of unbridled joy and innocence sparkling through a boyish, toothless grin as he spied the grandmother he hadn't seen in years. The look on my mother's face is an imprint in my memory like few others: two years of cruel silence, hurt, betrayal, misunderstanding, estrangement from her own daughters were now tributaries from the headwaters of her broken heart across the landscape of her face. Where once there was a determined, self-reliant brow, this unique heartbreak had loosened and humbled its edges, while a visible mix of happiness and sorrow spread across her features. Grandmother embraced her now taller grandson, and a mother searched the eyes of her youngest daughter for signs of reconciliation. I weep as I write this, as I feel the tenderness of that strange but true gift of a broken heart—a wound that has never fully healed.

The moment was transformational in my relationship with my mother, with myself, and with the woman of my future self, whom I was then so desperate to craft. It was also the moment, though I did not fully realize it then, that I bound myself to Lee as my spiritual teacher in an act of radical reliance, a bond forged in gratitude for the remorse that now humbles and softens my determination to do it my own way. Gratitude for the ferocity of his uncompromising demand on me, for his forbearance regarding the human condition, and for awakening that forbearance within me that now interpenetrates every day of my life.

The mind-shattering heartbreak that my guru spoke of, a heartbreak from which we hopefully never recover, begins the moment we choose to allow a tiny crack in our concept of right and wrong and in our attachment to who and what we thought we were. For me, this is the gift of a true guru, a gift more valuable than gold; a gift that is available to us all, no matter if we have a living guru pointing the way or if our guru is Christ, Allah, Buddha or our spiritual friend. When such a one nudges us, and indicates the way with a finger pointing to the moon, my advice is RUN, DON'T WALK! Act "as if" . . . Embody the vision of your future self; open to that shimmering world that is, as Rumi says, "too full to talk about," where "ideas, language, even the phrase 'each other' doesn't make sense anymore."

The moment I chose to stop, drop and go . . . to see my mother again . . . the Divine aligned Itself to meet me in that field on Orcas Island. There, anger, blame and judgment were transformed into delight, and a new relationship began with my mother's borderline eccentricities—her sibylesque Gemini, skeptic of skeptics, and crack-me-down, funny-wise woman—before pride could snatch away the chance.

TEN

The Name of Love

He who knows Love and her coming and goings
Has experienced and can understand
Why it is appropriate
That Hell should be the highest name of Love.
—HADEWIJCH OF ANTWERP,
13TH-CENTURY DUTCH MYSTIC

*I*t wasn't the fact that Hadewijch said this that troubled me but that I understood what she meant. More troubling still was when I read Mirabai, the fourteenth-century mad love-mystic who said: "Strange is the path / When you offer your love. / Your body is crushed at the first step. / If you want to offer love / Be prepared to cut off your head / And sit on it." At this point, I knew I was in over my head. Then I read novelist and poet D. H. Lawrence, who said in plainer English, "The best love stories come after the wedding . . . married relationships are damnably difficult." To which I said, *true dat, D.H!*

It has taken me nearly three decades of love in intimate and married relationships, colliding with my *bhakti* spiritual path, to begin to relax into what these mystics were entranced by. My first marriage, a depiction of romance and naiveté, was followed by a hot rebound and fated love affair; and my second marriage, also hot, has required the endurance of a triathlon.

∾

"Leo, Venus, Mercury all congregate in your Career House," my astrologer said, her words calling me to attention. "Your chart jumps right out at you and brags 'born to lead and succeed.'"

"No surprises so far," I said, seated comfortably in the swiveling ergonomic chair in my home office, my pedicured feet propped atop my desk.

"These three power planets are clustered together in a configuration equivalent to getting the king, queen and ace of the same suit in a poker hand. We see this lineup with the wealthiest, most successful business people in the world."

"Sounds promising," I said, feeling some justified pride. Our phone call continued as she commented further on my jackpot of career-money confluence and a bunch of things I had no fluency in at all: Ketu and Rahu, debilitated and rehabilitating planets.

"Saturn," she continued, "is in your ascendant with Libra—a planet Saturn takes kindly to. Lucky you, again," she said, as if I'd won the lottery.

The hour passed auspiciously while I made a mental note: *She has not mentioned relationships.* Curious. Was she a save-the-best-for-last kind of astrologer, or was she building the Dagwood of shit sandwiches? Was my Relationship House dilapidated so beyond repair that nothing short of a crane and wrecking ball would do? With cautious optimism I stated the obvious: "You haven't mentioned my Relationship House. What kind of shape is it in?"

A pause occupied the airwaves long enough for the Jeopardy jingle to come to mind.

"Well . . ." she said.

I cut her off at the pass, "*Well* is a loaded opener."

"We-ell," she dragged the interjection out as you might the tip of a splinter, pulling it ever so carefully from an infected wound to extract it whole. "Your Relationship House is, well, not well-developed. Let's say . . . it's not your strong suit. That's all."

"What would it take to remodel that house?"

"You will have your work cut out for you. It isn't going to be easy, but remodeled homes are often the homes we love the most in the end, aren't they?"

She sounded like a forthright Mr. Rogers, at once educating and reassuring: "Although the water washes down the bathtub drain and disappears, *you* will not be washed down with it— because *you* don't fit."

On a brisk Wednesday afternoon in mid-October of 2005, I landed at JFK, gathered my bags, and made my way posthaste to the rental car. With driving directions propped on the passenger's seat, I headed in the direction of the Catskill Mountains on the outskirts of Woodstock, New York. As the Big Apple receded in my rearview mirror, the contrived sprawl of concrete and steel yielding to uncultivated vegetation, the lazy days of summer appeared to be changing clothes for the chilly nights ahead. Autumn's variegated shades of color splattered the Northeast hillside, and the air was a distillate of peat, maple and hard cider. I arrived at my destination, a Buddhist retreat center, in the late afternoon. Parking the car, I took a deep, cleansing breath, noticing as I did the sensation of butterflies flapping against the inner walls of my chest.

I had crossed the country to attend the first "Gathering of Grandmothers"—a group of tribal elders from across the globe, thirteen of them—along with special guests Gloria Steinem, Francis Lapp and Tenzin Palmo, and ordinary women like me. Each was doing her part to remember the sacred, advocate for vanishing spiritual and tribal traditions, and protect herbal medicines and biodiversity from falling further into extinction through rainforest deforestation and the threat of climate change.

These weren't my only reasons for being there. Once again, that mischievous universal force had conspired to bring me on this particular pilgrimage to the very place where my divorce-papers-served second husband was living, and working as a caretaker.

Einstein once said that we cannot simultaneously prevent and prepare for war. While I was praying and advocating for humanity to return to sanity and end its war with nature, I was still at war within my eleven-year love affair. Having lost what was once sacred, I had turned what is precious and rare—the domain of love—into a war zone and hell.

The ace-high royal flush hand in my Career House and the mixed-suit twos and threes in my Relationship House were further complicated when I fell in love with and married an artist. Need I say more? If I do, I'll allow history to illustrate my meaning. Picasso's life and art consumed eight great loves. Dali was said to have been saved from his own madness by his wife, Gala. The artist pairing of Frida Kahlo and Diego Rivera was a tempest of pain and passion in their pursuit of love and art. The odds were not in my favor.

My husband Bruce—though it has taken me a hellishly long time to admit—is w-ell, borderlining on genius. But I forgive him for this because he can be funny as a pet monkey, and he has been easy on the eyes at every age. Blessed with a set of almond-shaped, Adriatic blue eyes, a perfectly sculpted nose, a gracious forehead framed by a standoffish hairline, and a perpetually sexy five o'clock shadow, Bruce has the rugged good looks of a young Clint Eastwood. Though I've never had his astrological chart done, I've deduced that he also has a plethora of planets in his Helpy Helperton house.

On the subject of helping, cooking meals is nonnegotiable for Bruce. He does all the cooking—both because he does not burn hard-boiled eggs, and because I'm a better eater than cooker.

Home, car and bike maintenance are his domain, too. These come free with the marriage, except for the attention I am required to pay as he narrates these helpful services with a tone of papal infallibility. He is responsible for the route plans that go with all our errands—the ETO, Errand Time Optimization—because alone I am an overly optimistic time estimator. And then there are the errand *lists*—of his making as well because of the fact that when I take in oxygen I also spend money. Some errands require more than a list; they require that we carry O2 tanks. Therefore, he takes care of all the domestic details.

In addition to being an artistic, ruggedly good-looking Helpy Helperton, the man I fell in love with is also a devotee of nature. He believes, with the whole of his being, that the "guru" is not another human being. The true guru is *us*, as our connection to nature. This is his cherished divinity, his dharma, and his refuge.

My dear husband's love of helping spills from this devotion to honor nature and from his own heart of sadness; sadness over humanity's disconnect from nature and the resulting loss to our collective soul. One who possesses such a heart, as he does, who feels this loss that many of us anesthetize and still remains willing to embrace his own darkness, as he does, is a soul that shines uncommonly bright. This is Bruce's true genius and beauty.

At some point along the path to my taking refuge in the dharma and guru and sangha, a strange thing happened, however. My beloved husband turned from heartfelt, Adriatic-eyed, nature lover to a know-it-all starving artist with a depressive worldview that reflected his attachment to the Four Horsemen of the Apocalypse. This is to say nothing about the gas mask that hangs in his office. After all, nothing says "Welcome to my world" quite like a gas mask!

Have you ever noticed that when someone we love morphs into the opposite of our desire, we morph into the opposite of theirs? Weird how that works, isn't it? Well, that is exactly what happened to us. The more he resembled Marlon Brando's crazed Colonel Kurtz in the classic film *Apocalypse Now*, the more I resembled a sanctimonious, spiritually combed-over anger junkie. Think Glenda the Good Bitch.

"It boils down to love," my teacher counseled me in his letter, in response to mine—the one where I wrote to inform him that I had made up my mind and was filing for divorce. "We've turned relationship into hell, and now with me having a guru—for Chrissake, he circles the wagons to 'kill the buddha on the road'—it's one more thing to argue about instead of the kindness, compassion and generosity I imagined my spiritual path bringing us. This is hell—not nirvana. I'm done!" I wrote, with Ms. Buck-Stops-Here leading the charge. To which Lee answered: "I have no words easy or otherwise, of advice. Each person knows their own bottom line. But I will say this, it's not about your Work [*as a student*]. You can work to my satisfaction in or out of the marriage. So do not make decisions on that basis. It boils down to love, not duty. And, you don't have to throw 'your guru' in his face, dominating shared spaces with reminders of [me, me, me]. Allow him to pray as he wishes, and you pray as you wish. Anything else is manipulation and pettiness. In any event, you have my regard, and attention."

∼

Back to Woodstock, two+ years later.

The butterflies took flight in a cramped corner of my stomach the moment I heard the *rap, rap, rap*. I opened the door to my room in the quaint, turn-of-the-century B&B where I was staying to see Bruce standing there in the flesh, after losing sight of him for much too long. Avoiding eye contact, and with an awkward cotillion curtsy, I waved him past me and into the room.

"Hey," I said, my awkwardness about as indiscreet as a tube top.

"Hi," he said, looking past my awkwardness and through me.

"Would you like something to drink?" I asked.

"No. I'm fine, thanks," he said, his eyes now taking refuge in me.

With one hand I bitchslapped myself to keep from admitting that he was more handsome than ever, while the other motioned to the bay window seat overlooking the street below, now turning into a monochrome of drizzle, damp, and dank. We each wedged into opposite ends of the window seating—me furtive and folding like a spider backing into a corner, he molding easy as Play-Doh.

He was leaner. Had he taken up cycling, or was that yoga I detected in his abs? His eyes were the same brilliant blue they had always been, though I didn't remember them to be so kind. *Hmm?* I thought. "How are you doing—you look well," I said, conscious that I was parsing every word I uttered, nervous and restrained.

"I'm good. You look beautiful," he blurted with a complete absence of the anger I was expecting—divorce-papers-served and all.

"Thanks, you as well," I said. "Have you taken up yoga?"

"No, not really. Caretaking again, I get plenty of exercise being outdoors, in nature. Some things never change," he said.

I searched his face and body language because something *had* changed, but *what* exactly I had not yet put my finger on. He was different, and it wasn't just his six-pack abs. Broken? Vulnerable? He looked broken, in a good way. Like the mirrors that must break when we are no longer clinging to images of the past. Like the caramelized glaze on creme brûlée, cracked with creamy goodness oozing up between the broken pieces, all caramely and crème fraîche.

It was a Sunday evening darshan, at his ashram in La Douce, France, when my guru gave a talk to the assembled crowd of devotees, students and visitors in which he strayed into the disputed ground of relationships on the path. I was there. I listened intently.

> Sometimes couples go into psychotherapy and realize that they got into the relationship for the wrong reasons, and they begin to question the basis of the relationship. I say: So what? If you are in love, who cares? If you are in love, protect what you have. My viewpoint is: Love matters; psychology does not matter . . . If you are in love in any way, you are a fool to allow your psychology to destroy that love—and it *can* destroy it, because love can be the strongest thing in the Universe, but it can also be extremely delicate. So if there is love, you want to protect it.

During the two-plus years that Bruce and I had spent apart, I'd shifted my love and devotion to guru, dharma and sangha. Being the A+-type, overachieving, approval-seeking, well-shod person that I am, I engaged the spiritual path with strategies for success, as I do with everything.

1. Identify the challenges and define vision.
2. Build trust and enroll others.
3. Implement policies, procedures and consistency.
4. Shop for devotional wear.

I engaged formal practice with the intent of a CEO determined to make a success of her business and, in time, despite my right choice for the wrong reasons, practice had its way with me.

Nothing replaces time-in with the practices of mindfulness and self-observation-without-judgment. Staying the course, they will reveal the tape loop of the mind and desire; and our ingrained habits will eventually be seen for all their . . . well, *loopiness*.

Since my judgment of others is, as it was pre-spiritual path, snarky and harsh, self-righteousness took on a whole new meaning once "spiritual student of a guru" was added to my CV. The darkness in me was being exposed, liberated from the binding shadows of my denial into the clear light of the dharma. As the eminent Tibetan Buddhist master Chögyam Trungpa Rinpoche once said, "By taking refuge [in guru, dharma, sangha], we are committing ourselves to freedom."

The pendulum swing of endless desire had tossed the whole of my colorful husband into the swamp of my own projections. I had lost sight of our love; and in time, thankfully, practice cultivated remorse and tossed me into a hellish longing. Longing to reconcile and reunite with my sweet-hearted lover, friend and helpmate and give love another chance.

❧

"I know this is going to sound crazy, but I miss doing his laundry," I said to my roommate Linda as I listlessly folded my limp towels and underpants one Saturday afternoon just before the Woodstock reunion.

"Yeah, you're right. It sounds crazy," Linda replied without hesitation.

"It does?" I said, seeking approval.

"Hell, yes! I wouldn't miss his laundry one bit, but his heart . . . that I'd miss and come to regret that I'd hung it out to dry if I had love like you have," she said, in her best Kentucky no- bullshit.

As my guru said, and I now know from experience, it boils down to love—not duty— and fiercely protecting that love. Rather than guarding and protecting the pocket where our love was hiding, Bruce and I became a couple of desperate street thieves filching from each other's pockets: this psychological quirk, that illusory belief, this lack of surrender and that failure to serve threw differences and imperfections in the other's face as if proof that he, or she, was a fraud and unworthy of love.

I have learned the hard way that the single most transformative human emotion is remorse—that authentic regret we've all felt at one time or another for our unconscious actions that caused our lover pain. Having glimpsed ourselves without our mask of blame or guilt or shame, Bruce and I have stood naked in remorse's light, one-hundred percent responsible for the mess we've each made.

Taking refuge in the dharma provided, for me, a context for living that has served as a meeting with my shadow and the gift of remorse, the consummation of which gives birth to genuine forgiveness, compassion and gratitude.

My stars have made my Relationship House what it is—a remodel job from hell! So I've accepted this fact, stopped remodeling, and begun incanting a mystical spell of my own over my relationship with Bruce, which we renewed before the ink had a chance to dry on the divorce papers. It goes like this: Lose sight of psychology—the you and me. Break that mirror! Go deeper and listen. Can you hear your longing calling? You fools, don't you know that only laughter and kindness and praise protect the fierce curve of love, Hell be its damnably high name.

ELEVEN

My Father's Daughter

Yes? No.
No? Yes.
Is there such a thing as paradox?
Only Mother and Father.
—LEE LOZOWICK, *DEATH OF A DISHONEST MAN*

As I write this, it is my birthday, and at my age I've almost mastered the art of forgetting it until cards, phone calls, emails, and of course text messages start arriving, reminding me more than any gift I could receive of how loved I am. When I was very young, my birthday was a day on which I felt an uncomplicated, unquestioned love. It was a day I could count on spending with my father.

July 1965—a Saturday. I was turning six that month. My father was scheduled to pick up my sister and me for his weekend with us. Every nerve in my body felt the way the wings of a June bug vibrating on a screen door sounds. Waiting for him to arrive was a torture worse than waiting for the school recess bell to ring. I pestered my mom in thirty-second intervals, like a trained parrot: "When will he get here, Mom? When will he get here, get here—Dad gunna get here?!" My sandaled feet padded the living room floor, my fingernails were chewed to stubs, and my eyes were trained on the street beyond the limbs of the humongous fig tree that looked like the limbs of a tarantula menacing above our driveway. At first sight of his car pulling sluggishly up the street and inching onto our drive, the screen door met the mitt of my hand, springing it wide as I shot clean through. My own spidery legs bicycled the air off the porch like the cartoon character Road Runner spinning his feet. I was down the front walk and, with a leap, hurled myself at my dad, who emerged from behind the wheel of his one-size-too-small convertible. Like a leech, I attached myself to him—every daughter-cell in my body collapsing in relief into the security of his strong and loving arms.

My father was a good-natured, generous, life-of-the-party sort—everyone from the gas station attendant to the restaurant maître d' knew him by "Charlie," and he called them by name too, each one seeming to be a best friend. He'd introduce my sister and me to each and all with a dignity and pride I could not have named but always felt, and always using our proper names, "Mary Susan and Kristen Carol—my daughters." He was Santa Claus and the ice-cream man rolled into one: a robust, barrel-chested figure with a bulbous, veiny nose that reminded me of that funny guy from the Kellogg's Corn Flakes commercials, Jimmy Durante; only my father was way funnier. He had a penchant for the finer things in life that exceeded his motivation for earning the money to pay for them. This landed him at the betting window of the Santa Anita racetrack almost every weekend, inevitably landing my sister and me there, too, on those winsome weekend visits. Perched on the deck of his broad knee with an icy-cold Roy Rogers—that cherry-coke kid cocktail—gripped in our tiny fists, my sister and I would wait for my father to call out horse names from the track form. "*Kings Ransom*? *Pony Up*? Girls, waddaya think of *In the Black*? Oh look, Mary Susan, how about *Shanghai Sue*? Do you have a good feeling about that one?" We'd giggle and bugle out a name as if we were miniature mediums, then retrieve the maraschino cherry from our drinks like it was a treasure from a pirates' chest and suck the sugary fruit from its stem. Our limbs wrapped around him, heads arching back in peals of laughter, teeth and gums bared, howling at our father's smallest gesture; picture a family of contented monkeys tangled together, picking fleas off one another. We were in love and lost to all but him.

These cherished memories are few. Weekends with my father were postponed until Christmas shortly after that year, and alternate birthdays became the extent of my relationship with my father until those eroded into cards, then were eclipsed by benign neglect as the self-discovery of my teen years unspooled into a forty-year string of absences. As I write this, my father has been dead for four years—seven years after he came to town . . . Oh, forgive me, I left out the part about how he spent his last years in Prescott, Arizona, close to the only family willing and able to care for him.

∽

"We need to get Dad out of there," my sister said, urgent-sounding on the other end of the line. "He's got heart failure and he needs open heart surgery. He's eighty years old and been living with Uncle Louie and Aunt Tillie for years. Tillie hates Dad, always has, because he's the Grand Poobah of couch potatoes, and they're a bunch of old farts who can't help each other anymore."

My sister, who changed her name about the same time I did—from Mary Susan to Diva—is all pioneer woman and elbow grease on matters of how-to and who-to; she is bullwhip and spiked heels. If something needs getting done, Diva is our gal. The rest of the story of how my dad got to town is a blur. Diva moved him to her downstairs apartment—an hour from my home. Then, in short order, he had open heart and prostate surgeries, reluctantly went to his prescribed rehab at a local gym and returned daily to the couch from whence he came . . . until two years later, when I got another call.

"I'm so freakin' done with him. His doctor says his heart is like new, but it takes an Act of Congress to get him off that goddamn couch. You deal with him! I did my part." My sister rightfully asserted her position just before she announced her detailed plans for "packing his shit and moving him into an apartment in Prescott" just minutes away from me and my mother, leaving him in our collective care. "Fair enough, you've done your part," I said, gratefully, gulping back the thousand questions surfacing from a well of uncertainty.

Fast forward two years to a chilly Friday morning in November. It was about nine o'clock. I had been home less than twelve hours after a week on the road and was settling in at my desk, cozy in my fleece boots and sipping a morning beverage, when the phone rang. I pushed the button on my headset with one hand while the other remained affixed to the mug as I smuggled another sip and answered. "Hello?"

"Is Tarini Weaver there?"

With some reluctance at the mismatch of names, I 'fessed up. "Yes," I said, as I knocked back another sip in mid-sentence. "This is she."

"Hi . . . This is the Yavapai Regional Medical Center. We have your father, Charles. He asked me to call you to come pick him up." The call catapulted me out of my morning ritual. Just before I left on my business trip, my mother and I had taken him to the hospital, where he was admitted for severe shortness of breath.

"Okay. I'm leaving now," I said. "Please tell him I'll be there in about fifteen minutes."

"He'll be waiting for you," she said.

Upon arrival, I saw my dad seated in a wheelchair surrounded by nurses. "How do you do it, Dad? You have every woman in the joint doting on you, hand and foot. It must be your charisma because God knows it's not your jogging suit!" I joked, while a short, dark-haired nurse seated behind her station officiously shoved release papers in front of me and downloaded information about his stay: tests they ran, how he fared, prescriptions written. With half my attention listening to her report, the other half was making a mental note of my father's good-natured patience even as he slouched beneath an aura of resignation that belied his usually jovial demeanor. I gathered his belongings, wrapped in a plastic bag held atop his lap, and noticed his odor and his clothes, in that order. His sweatpants were urine-stained to the knees, identifying the source of the offending odor, and his sweatshirt resembled a graffiti canvas sprayed in meatloaf with gravy and splattered with raspberry jam. A standing nurse with platinum-dyed hair and powder-blue eye shadow pulled me a compassionate distance aside and asked if I had "brought any other clothes for him."

"No," I said, instantly regretful.

"I hate to send him home like this, but these were the only clothes he had," she said, with concern for his dignity. As quickly as embarrassment flushed my face in strawberry-colored patches, gratitude for her kindness washed them out to a humbled pink blush.

"We'll be heading straight home," I said. "Thank you for your caring."

∼

My father was a Navy veteran who proudly served his country in WWII, more out of a sense of duty and the "right thing to do" than out of political convictions. "That is what you did back then; serve your country," he'd say with pride.

The *SS Enterprise* was the name of his ship. I know this not only because he had an elephant's memory when it came to details of the war, but also because his favorite ball cap had the name boldly embroidered on its brim. He never left home without it. I could never predict when another old vet—maybe with one lung, or an amputated limb—at the VA hospital might recognize the name of my dad's ship and strike up a conversation with him while we waited for a prescription. My dad was an encipherer in the Navy, that guy who deciphered and transmitted messages by invisible ink and code language, shuttling messages back and forth across enemy lines.

Though my dad spoke fondly about his time in the service, he was an outspoken Democrat, vocal in his opposition to war, in particular the wars in Iraq and Afghanistan. His contempt of ex-president Bush and "his cronies' crimes against humanity" was clear. As he put it, "Bush and Cheney ought to be put away for what they've done to those countries and millions of innocent people!" My dad voted for Hillary Clinton over Barak Obama, though "either one would bring much-needed change," he argued. "The first woman or black man in the White House is an historical moment I never imagined I'd live to see." Everyone from the Senior Day Care director to the nurse who helped me get him into the car that morning, despite his homeless vibe, all commented on how "sweet" my dad was.

Although this family reunion with my father after forty years was not his idea, he didn't put up a fight against it. In fact, I learned, my dad was rarely argumentative and always courteous . . . especially when someone was offering him a bed, or their couch, and three meals a day. He was a positive, uncomplaining, and kind soul. Regardless of who initiated the reunion, had my dad and I not been reacquainted I would have gone to my grave believing my story about him: a deadbeat couch potato with whom I had absolutely nothing in common. My story was only partly true.

At the age of five, when my dad's mother and father could no longer afford to feed him, he was left at a Catholic orphanage. There he was educated and sheltered until he was thirteen. This enlightening fact put my relationship with my dad in a whole new light, as it did my own fears about parenting and difficulties sustaining relationships. My dad's deep grief and profound shame became evident in his nearly total lack of self-care, or, to be less diplomatic, his sloth.

"Jeezus, Mary, and Joseph! We need to cut those finger- and toenails, Dad. You're a lethal weapon!"

"What, these?" my dad said, holding up his ten ghoulish-looking fingers. "I've got to have something to defend myself with at my age. What if that old bag next door broke into my room and tried to steal all my money?"

"Dad, that old bag next door can barely walk to the mailbox. She's the least of your worries. I'd be more worried about this dish under your chair. Its contents look menacing," I said, as I pulled a half-eaten burrito from underneath the Barcalounger and stratified newspapers, suggesting that he'd taken a nap and wanted to save the rest for later. Spoonfuls of peanut butter, parched as adobe clay, lay in odd places around his house, as if the phone had rung and startled him in mid-bite and with the one spry body function he had left—reflex—he'd flung the spoon, half-eaten peanut butter and all, clear across the room.

"I'm gunna . . . *whatever* . . . later," was my father's personal brand, a sort of reverse psychology strategy from Nike's wildly successful "Just Do It."

"Hey, Dad, how's your 'Gunna Do It' strategy working for you?"

"Oh, it's working just fine," he countered. "I have no end to 'Gunna Do It' ideas. Nike oughta call me and I'll share some of 'em—at a good price, of course."

Being a devotee of a Buddhist-hybrid spiritual path, one who has taken a vow closely akin to that of the Bodhisattva, didn't mean I had to suffer silently and ignore the opportunity to bring levity to the task when my father provided such damn good material. "I've got a million-dollar idea of my own, Dad. You know that laundry in your closet? Well, it's turned into The Blob. I suggest doing it before it oozes out, does you in, and then steals all your money."

∾

This kind of sarcasm from me is usually a red herring. In the case of my dad, I used it to divert attention from my disappointment in him as a father figure to my sister and me, and from seeing him in truth, as he was—an agreeable and unkempt slouch, the metaphor for his unremarkable-in-every-way life. As uncomfortable as it was to be with him at times, accepting him *as he was*, with the years of grief and shame composting him into the couch, enabled me to trace the roots of my judgments of him, and of anyone, for that matter, who doesn't do for themselves what they are able to do. Like those who choose to blame others, something, anything, for why they can't do X, Y or Z. They might blame parents, the government, the economy, global warming, God, and invoke that ultra-lame blame, "because . . . (fill in the blank)."

My father was the czar of such blame, both of others and about things he wanted to do but "couldn't, because . . . ": "I always wanted to go to Egypt, but I . . ." ; "If I could have taken that tour of duty in China during the war . . . ." Hearing yet another excuse, I slapped verbal handcuffs on my sarcastic mouth that otherwise would have liberated the smart ass inside my mind that wanted to say, "Dad, you aren't in heaven *yet*, so how 'bout you get off that goddamn couch and go to the park with me and people watch. Who knows, you might meet someone there from Egypt, or China!"

Instead, I listened to his story for the gazillionth time—the one where he was offered a second tour in the Navy, to be stationed in China, but turned it down and returned to the States, where he met my mother. "The rest is history," he'd start in, and finish off with "I never should have married her . . . she made me do it, you know." Then he'd gaze out the window of his disheveled room as if the fabulous life he would have lived was a movie being projected on a screen only he could see. It was here, at the junction of my coming to know that my dad was orphaned, his inability to be a competent father, and his litany of gunna-do-its that the dharma cast its compassionate light on him, and on similarities in my own life.

"Dad, why did your dad move away, leaving your mother alone with five kids she couldn't afford to feed and then had to put in an orphanage?" I asked.

"He went to find work . . . my father was a hard-working man who everyone loved," he'd said.

"*Really* . . . so why didn't he send her money to support you all when he did find work?" I said, leaning into the credulity of his story and not hiding my judgment.

"I wish I had asked my mother some of those questions—I do. But my mother and father loved us, and so did those nuns. The nuns were hard on us, but they were good to us," he said, at once sharing his feelings and exposing, ironically, his basic goodness—his Buddha nature.

Despite my father's absenteeism and colossal inertia, these brief encounters with him in those last years filled in large gaps in our relationship. Having my father with me for this short time, with me at an age where I had gained some perspective, I was given the gift of getting to know him, of learning in small bits the kind of loss and heartache and pain that was the glue that patched him together.

"If we hope to go to another 'octave' in our spiritual lives—to mature on the path—more often than not it boils down to something as simple as healing with our parents," my guru said in an evening talk during this period when I was getting to know my father. Lee's words seared into my memory like a branding iron.

Maturity, for me, meant letting go of *my* agenda and simply enjoying the gift of being with my father, not recapitulating the past or demanding, childishly, to "get my needs met" as a grown woman. Neither did it mean attempting to change him. It meant not gagging (or at least not hurling) at the smell from pissed pants or soiled diapers tossed to the bathroom floor and left for me or my mother to pick up. In dropping my agenda as completely as I could, I learned that my father was as simple a man as I will ever know—a man who never demanded more than was given, ate whatever was served, was good humored, and was tolerant of others, despite his chronic pain and the inconveniences of old age such as heart disease and adult diapers.

"Dad, we're coming to get you to take you to dinner tonight, remember? Be sure to shower before we come. Spruce up a bit! Who knows, we might meet some hot Granny. Heck, she may even be Chinese."

"Okay, sweetheart, I'll see you later. I love you." Click. The sound of an abrupt dial tone rang harsh in my ear, truncating an unexpected moment of true intimacy from my father, leaving me hanging, suddenly aware of both an authentic gratitude for the moment and my tendency to want more. Just as suddenly, I heard the call to practice—to invoke my dad's Buddha nature of "receiving what is given without complaint," and to be grateful for the simple and unquestioned love my dad was offering.

While waiting in the lobby of the lab for some routine blood work, I was thumbing a large-print *Readers Digest* article on heart-healthy do's and don'ts when a Rumpelstiltskin-looking old man hobbled through the door. Although there were a couple dozen empty seats to choose from, the man collapsed in the seat next to mine and, without pause, leaned into my personal space, exhaling the smell of the nearly dead, and said, "Don't get old, it's not for sissies."

"I feel you," I replied, smiled good-naturedly into his tired eyes, then returned to reading my article on the anti-aging benefits of omega-3 fish oils with the zeal of the newly converted.

TWELVE

Everything Is Broken

"You know, Hobbes, some days even my lucky
rocket ship underpants don't help."
—BILL WATTERSON, CREATOR OF *CALVIN & HOBBES*

*T*he dharma is considered a jewel—a gem
whose radiance illuminates any flaw in our beliefs, any nick
in our certainty or blemish in our sanctity, protecting us as it
does from becoming lost in illusion or believing our own lies.
As the great troubadour poet-cum-Zen master Leonard Cohen
once said, "There is a crack in everything, that is how the light
gets in."

Heartbreak is a mystical crack through which Divine
Influence—*light*, if you like—can enter. That formless, nameless luminosity penetrates the broken heart not to shoo the
blues away like roaches in daylight but to widen the crack so
that even more light can reveal the beauty hiding in everything, cockroaches and all.

∾

"I hate to be the bearer of bad news, but from the x-rays it looks like we'll have to extract three teeth and do a bone graft in your jaw," my dentist said.

Angry!

"Honey, I didn't want to tell you this, but they are foreclosing on my home," my mother said over the phone.

"What do you mean, Mom?"

"I didn't want to worry you, but I applied for refinance through the Obama program and have provided the banks with everything, and now I've been denied. They're going to foreclose."

"When?"

"Sixty days."

Powerless!

∾

It was the first week of January on a Friday afternoon when the caller ID on my cell phone announced Sam calling. When my twenty-seven-year-old son living 1,500 miles away calls, it's a welcome surprise. "Hey, Sam," I said cheerfully. "What's up?"

The response from his end followed a noticeable lag. Then, as if he were second-guessing a word choice in Scrabble, he blundered, "Uh, Mom—uh—I . . ." It wasn't so much the fact that he was speaking with a stutter that alerted my mothering instinct as it was the dread in his tone and the tremble of his cadence.

"Sam, is everything okay, hon?"

"No. Actually. I have some really bad news."

"What, what? What is it, Sam?" I was stuttering now, as panic choked my words. My mind leapfrogged ahead to an image of "really bad news" that I could manage: a wrecked car, maybe he lost his job, or his girlfriend broke up with him—my son's first heartbreak. How will I console him? Each of these options ricocheted around my mind in the time it took for Sam to speak next. Without preamble he said, "Tyler died last night from an overdose of heroin."

It's strange how a sentence of mostly monosyllabic words can arrest time and shove Earth's revolutions into hard reverse; how those retrograde moments can divorce our personal universe from gravitational law. Short of getting a call from Tyler to tell me my son died last night from an overdose of heroin, the impact of hearing my son's voice telling me that his best friend of twenty years (the child who was as close to a second son as I will ever know) died last night, from any cause, was heartrending.

Dreamlike flashes of Tyler's last moments—the suffering, the inability to protect him from the consequence—began slamming doors on careers, weddings, grandkids. Life instantly reeled out from its neatly wound spool the way a fly-fishing line unwinds—out into a dystopian dream that is the stuff reserved for the movies.

That my son had found his best friend dead and then needed to be the messenger delivering to me the second worst call this mom could receive was eclipsed only by the call I would learn Sam had made to Tyler's mom and dad to break the same really bad news. My body collapsed to the ground like a thermometer shattering and spilling its mercury. I hit bottom in a pool of grief.

Heartbreak!

"Accept what is, as it is, here and now" is a recommended practice that I've been given to help me navigate the uncertain path of life, a practice which continues to move me to seek refuge in the dharma. This jewel of practice is a tool that offers practical protection from the perils of the illusion of permanence or, said another way, from the mind's addiction to pretending not to know the truth. In the beginning, the tool is a scythe we clumsily swing to hack at the weeds of pretense, inauthenticity, fantasy, and the beliefs we cling to, hoping to maintain our perceptions of self and other, and of reality. Over time, with the refinement that comes with conscious attention, the tool becomes a samurai sword that we wield against the roots of illusion—those mirages responsible for the misery and suffering we cause ourselves and others when we reject what is. Impermanence is *what is*.

My traffic tickets, dental reconstructions, and relationship challenges were like Little League in the domain of practice with "what is, as it is." Where death was concerned, I'd had little preparation, other than with my guru's death, which I quickly tossed into the "there is no death" category, telling myself all the spiritual mumbo-jumbo that bypassed reality as it is. He died. I missed him.

When the news of Tyler's death struck, sudden and stark, reality hit hard. I pulled my samurai sword from its sheath and started wielding. In other words, I cried. Truth be told, I wailed. I wailed loud and long enough for neighbors to hear, and I didn't care. And with every wail I felt a bit of Tyler's parents' pain. Being a mother, I then began to feel a bit of the grief of every other mother who has lost a son to drugs or alcohol, or way too soon. I then felt myself wailing with every Jewish mother, and her Palestinian counterparts on the other side of the illusory walls of "mine and yours." Then Rwandan and Somalian and Bosnian moms, and the collective of mothers throughout history who have ever suffered such tragic loss of their children. The levy broke. The crack in me widened; an ocean of unshed tears gushed out and light crept in. When I was spent of tears, I arose from that pool of grief, forever changed by these losses, a shattered and lighter being.

Mourning!

∾

In the gaping emptiness of Tyler's bedroom, Sam and I stood with his bereaved father, mother and sister, our heads bent like Zen students bowing in reverence to the dignity in the other, while our tears fell in hard droplets to the blood-stained carpet beneath our feet. Our arms laced together formed an intergenerational tapestry, our love for Tyler, the thread that had brought us together years ago, now being woven into an inextricable bond holding us together.

Before his parents arrived, Sam and I had packed Tyler's closet of clothes, folded laundry left behind in his hamper, moved furniture his family requested we donate to Habitat for Humanity, boxed books, and separated what seemed important and personal, doing what little we could to prepare the room.

As we worked, Sam and I shared our grief and a few surprises. "Hey Sam, Tyler did some interesting reading, huh? *Hitchhiker's Guide to the Galaxy?*"

"Yeah," said Sam. "He was always quoting some crazy shit or other from there. I want to keep that one."

"Here's something on mindfulness meditation," I said. "And he even has this book, *What Makes You Not a Buddhist*, by Khyentse Rinpoche. This is one of my favorites."

"He was into all kinds of world religion stuff," Sam said, as I cracked open the modest blue book by the Rinpoche, heading straight to some dog-eared pages.

"Do you know if Tyler read this?" I asked, looking more closely at some underlined passages.

"I think he got it from you, Mom. He attributed his interest in alternative religion stuff to you, and my dad."

"How's that, Sam?"

"Well, you know he felt you both were so loving and generous and kind, and . . . well—your Buddhist stuff. It made him question and want to explore other beliefs and religions."

"Hmm," I said aloud, then allowed Sam's words to fall heavily, as though Tyler were telling me so himself.

"Sam, look here. It appears he underlined some passages in the chapter titled, 'Everything Is Emptiness.' Do you think it would be okay if I took this with me to read again?" I said, while Sam continued to box up more books.

"Yes, Phil said for me to keep whatever meant something to me. I'm sure Tyler would be happy to know you had the book, Mom."

I took the 130-page book home that night to my room and reread it cover to cover. The dog-eared section on emptiness drew my memory to the Heart Sutra—that dharmic riddle about emptiness and form. Being the Buddhist hybrid that I am, I've encountered the sutra more than once and can attest that, in the wake of inconsolable sorrow, it forced its way into my awareness like an untreated toothache.

The sutra shouts its crazy wisdom at us like a town crier standing in the village square clanging a discordant bell: "Gone, gone, gone beyond—gone, altogether beyond—oh what an awakening, all hail!" I cannot be sure about the "beyond" or the "awakening" the sutra hails, but standing together with Sam and Tyler's family in Tyler's emptied room that day, I woke to the emptiness of form: table, chair, bed, computer, concert posters, and two human parents, brokenhearted and emptied by unspeakable grief.

An uncomfortable slurry of emotions welled up inside me that I was not prepared to reconcile: pain over Tyler's suffering in silence; recognition of the suffering imposed on those who remain, left to meet the days and nights ahead without him; fear of death and its randomness, and the utter terror this stirs in me. Pissed at heroin, angry at shame, joyful and grateful for having known him, I was still helpless to ease the pain his parents now suffered. Yet I felt hopeful that if I practiced accepting what is, as it is, here and now, I would empty myself of the burning desire to fix what could not be fixed, and make more room in me to hold even a small measure of humanity's pain.

Sorrow!

∾

Some years back I was visiting with a sangha friend, catching up after her return to Arizona from a summer spent in Europe with our guru. On that day I was feeling hopelessness. Mary said that my feelings were in good company, then offered up a story of her own. Interestingly, during her time with him, Lee had said something that directly addressed my feeling: "We have to practice in the face of hopelessness or we have no business being on this earth . . . to do otherwise would be to turn our backs on the Divine."

"That's romantic sounding, Mary," I said, with an extra dose of snark. "But out here in the real world, everything is broken. I'm here to report that it's pretty hopeless."

She listened, so I went on. "Seriously, what is the point to all the practice, Mary? We practice in the morning, practice in the evening, practice all over this world, and when we finish with that practice there's a big pile of practice *out back* that needs to be done. And the suffering is unending." Then I proceeded to list all the things that are broken: "Global warming is melting the polar ice cap; species are falling to extinction faster than any other extinction in recorded history; there are tsunamis, hurricanes, volcanoes, cancer, corporate greed so colossal and insatiable that it took down the economy, and not a soul went to prison! And that's just *this* morning's headlines."

With genuine empathy, Mary responded to my rant. "Tarini, you are on to something. The dharma is intended to wake us from our sleep so we can no longer maintain the illusion. The human condition *is* heartbreaking, and it's damn difficult to bring ourselves to practice when we meet hopelessness on the path, as you are now. I can relate. Twenty-some years on the path and I feel I'm only just beginning, and anything I thought I knew was all self-importance."

I was touched by Mary's honesty and encouragement, and knew the truth in her words, but I wasn't finished venting. "I was so sure when I came to this school that I had what it takes to be liberated, freed from my neurotic, egoic suffering. As I look around now at the lives of sangha friends, I see that we are all habitual creatures, while humankind's insatiable greed for power takes down the planet with us on it. Fat chance for my liberation! I don't mean to wax apocalyptic and all, *I'm just sayin'*."

"This might just be cause for celebration, Tarini." Mary wasn't laughing.

"Yeah, I know." I paused, then continued. "I remember Carl Jung too. He said we should pull out the champagne when we finally hit bottom, because then we have a place to begin."

"It's a real beginning," Mary said, "to come this far and meet hopelessness and ask ourselves what we are doing here in spiritual life. Every one of us must be authentic and choose the right thing for the right reasons. To find oneself in the situation you are now in, and to choose to do as Lee is recommending—to offer praise and gratitude in the face of hopelessness—would be remarkable. We have come to know firsthand that what we have been given, the dharma, is a jewel; it is pristine and enduring, capable of shattering every illusion."

"It's the only choice, Mary, and I know it," I said, decidedly sobered. "My 'inner devotee' and my 'lover of God' are one-hundred percent in on the deal, but my 'renegade student' wants to celebrate my maturity with a glass of wine and lose myself in a mindless bestseller!"

Heartbreak is certain. It happens imperceptibly over time. Our childhood dog or a cousin we played with as a child dies. A rejection letter comes from a college we had our heart set on attending. We are passed over for a job. A relationship fails . . . or two or three. Our parent dies when we are too young to understand but old enough to feel their absence and experience loss. By the time we reach adulthood we have accumulated breaks and wounds and scar tissue that become the glue that binds together the scrapbook of our life.

Death was not a theme in my scrapbook. I had an uncle who died at thirteen, but he was too sick from leukemia to play with me much, and too spoiled (I thought) for me to want to play with him. I was too young to feel any great loss, though I observed my grandmother experience hers.

I sustained blows of neglect from my father who hung the moon, then slipped quietly out of orbit. The parent who took his place was the clichéd drunk and the abusive stepfather who violated boundaries of innocence and took his pound of flesh. This double whammy made lasting impressions.

My childhood romances left nicks and cracks. Then, *wham*, my son was born—a blow that turned the neglect, abuse and childhood disappointments into the wound that only God could heal. That wound opened up in divorce. A mother-daughter feud infected the wound, and remorse gave it a good scrub. A best friend got cancer, and as she wasted to near death, fear and helplessness tried to cauterize it. Instead, like salt, love tenderized it. My love affair of twenty years with my husband is aging the wound and seasoning it with each moment we open to love over and against the many ways we have available to protect ourselves from it. Then my guru died, followed closely by this young, bright life—Tyler's—so close and too soon. With these fatal blows to an irreparably fractured heart, Divine Influence now has a sliver of space to shine through.

The news report announces that a Palestinian child was shot at point-blank range by an Israeli as her parents watched. Amazingly, they choose love in the form of forgiveness instead of retaliation. Salty tears well up from my own raw heart for their stunning example of accepting *what it, as it is* with dignity big enough for the pain and luminosity of all humanity.

THIRTEEN

Travel with Guru and Sangha

Or, *What You Won't Find in Fodor's Travel Guide*

> It is as old as the stones.
> It came with Humans to the Earth
> and it offers them a way out
> of the web of sorrows
> but at a price:
> we must observe ourselves . . .
>
> —RED HAWK, *THE WAY OF POWER*

*M*e: "I'm looking forward to the India trip, Lee."

Lee: "India will be a hoot as long as you keep your raging sense of humor!"

∼

Before I left on the trip to India I heard someone say that India is a *feeling* country and America is a *thinking* country. Having made the trip, I agree with this assessment, though I might say it this way: India is woman and America is man.

It was the great Russian mystic G.I Gurdjieff who used the phrase "the Work" to signify the way to *seeing Reality*. Mr. Gurdjieff went on to define this Work business as a "masculine" affair, a hero's journey. You know, the stuff of cajones, with zero tolerance for excuses, blame, and whining. On the other hand, as my own spiritual master repeatedly pointed out, to live our human experience whilst doing *our Work*, and to live with a degree of dignity and a measure of emotional intelligence, is a feminine affair. "The Work" requires self-discipline, rigorous self-honesty, and a good spine; while living in relationship with others and life *as it is* requires generosity, kindness, forbearance, an open mind and a listening ear. In sum: we've got to lean in to this Work like a motherfucker *and* relax into life in the same breath.

Being that I have a Type-A All-American Achiever and a Compulsive Driver in the mandala of characters that make up my personality, the leaning-in part comes naturally to me, but the relaxing, the resting in the feminine (the Woman) that India proved to be, not so much! I see now that long before I set foot on the tarmac in Chennai my trip to India was a cosmically ordained encounter with this feminine principle.

Me: "So what was all that *about*, Lee? I don't know what to say, think or do about India at the moment. Was it the kind of thing one needs to do more than once to 'get it'? Or should I chalk this up to 'been there—done that'?" I was speaking to my guru in the Heathrow airport on our layover from Chennai to Phoenix while we shared an extra-greasy order of comfort food: bacon.

Lee: "No. There is no need to go back if you don't want to, and as for *what it was all about*—time will tell. Maybe it was nothing but a trip to India." The grin on his face widened in such a way that my mind jumped to conclude that he knew something he wasn't saying.

"I swear on a stack of Bhagavad Gitas I'll never go back to India" I said to someone who asked me about the trip soon after my return. It has been more than a decade now, and I have not returned to India . . . as I swore I would not. But, all things considered, should the circumstance present itself again, I would do *anything* in my power to take that trip.

The trip was a pilgrimage that Lee had made almost every year for more than twenty years with an entourage of his students to visit his teacher, Yogi Ramsuratkumar, the Beggar Saint of Tiruvannamalai. On this excursion in December of 2003, I was one of those students, although I would not meet the saint who my guru called his Father, his Sweetheart, Mad Trickster, and Dirty Beggar—among other names. The Yogi had died three years earlier. I would visit the old master's ashram, however, and meet the devoted women who served at his side for more than two decades, and who continue serving his work to this day. I walked with these women of devotion on the sacred ground where the Beggar Saint himself walked, and where he blessed countless other pilgrims who had made the trip to receive his darshan—including my teacher Lee, who the saint came to call his "son."

I don't think it was any secret to my guru, although I disguised it from myself for some time, that I came to India filled with hope that I would have an "awakening" event, some instant Kundalini Rising experience, like spiritual jumper cables to my dead chakras; or, at the very least, that I'd get the big *Wow* about my guru's guru—Yogi Ramsuratkumar—and learn what it was about this particular saint that had caused Lee to fall madly in love to the degree that his life was annihilated by it. Lee, a confessed "arrogant," "dishonest," and "self-interested" man, wrote hundreds of devotional poems to and for his beloved master. What kind of love could have moved such a self-described man to keep pace with this all-consuming muse?

Imagine, dear reader, my guru's dedication to his master and generosity to us, which involved traveling to India, one of the most chaotic places on the globe, with an entourage of thirty or forty students, each of whom brought excess baggage filled with clothes, vitamins, water bottles, and a full spectrum of annoying-as-hell habits. Actually, "habits" is too weak a word. Make that "demands"—for special food, daily exercise, Internet access, regular and personal attention *from the guru*, shopping, sleeping, carving out personal space, a clean restroom. No person in his or her right mind would choose to make such a trip a second time, but, amazingly, Lee did it over and over. It's a little like childbirth—it defies logic why women do it a second, and sometimes ten, times! But that is the point: such is the province of the heart.

I'd like to make it perfectly clear up front: these trips were not sight-seeing tours through the ashrams of India with our guru as travel guide. Five-star Indian resorts with hot showers and room service were in another India—one we never saw.

This pilgrimage was the guru's way of providing us with the perfect conditions for "the Work"—that uncomfortable stuff we don't know how to do, and which doesn't come naturally. For me, that would include travel to anywhere in groups larger than three or four other sweaty devotees, crammed in stinky buses, swaddled in yards of fabric, sleeping on cement floors. Relationship, as we've established, is not my strong suit. Don't get me wrong, I love people, and I am a people person. And I love my sangha (the community of devotees who have taken refuge in the dharma and the guru). They are the third jewel of refuge on the path (and decidedly my most tarnished). Still, I get fidgety and itchy and can't sustain the big group dynamic, especially where group mind, group think and group speak are inevitable and incestuous and invasive. I bolt, like veggies in too much heat, racing to go to seed. And, well, said another way, I fear intimacy. Yet, this is the push-pull and the jewel of sangha for those like me: to have people in my life who share my love of the dharma and the guru—kindred spirits who know the joys, insights, challenges, pitfalls, struggles and sorrows of the life of refuge on the path, and who are able to encourage me when I'm down, remind me when my poser is showing, and help me remember my purpose. I can't imagine life without refuge in sangha.

Had I read the fine print about the *Work* involved in the trip ahead, I may have scheduled that colonoscopy I keep putting off. But, as we have also established, I don't read manuals or the fine print. I was committed, and once committed I know how to "man up" to a challenge. I determined to do my work, at least for those eighteen days, in order to be with the guru and the sangha, to get some answers about Lee's guru, and to put another toe in the water of his world.

The "guru's world" is not a place. It is a ground of being that exists as love, expressed as the feminine pole of creation, in life—a force I would call *grace*. A gentle strength, clear-eyed discrimination, receptivity, tolerance, forbearance . . . I think you get my drift. Although it is the aim of the devotee, entering the guru's world and sustaining life at this refined altitude is tricky. Here is where the conscious work of self-observation and letting go come in—those moment-to-moment processes whereby we get to see our need for control, power over others, competition, greed, jealousy, pride, and then to release it all.

Self-observation and letting go will effect a radical shift— from a controlled, masculine, me-centered existence to one that inheres in the feminine, in grace, where concern for and attention to "other" is the culvert that directs life's flow. To undertake such work, to enter the guru's world when all the forces of habit and the status-quo culture seem to be directing otherwise, is to make an enormous leap of faith.

I made it a point to observe my guru on this trip the way an ornithologist observes birds in their natural habitat: silently taking notes. On bus rides, I observed, as he sat quietly—a renunciate of the small talk most of us engaged in to pass the time—that he was content; though I would not say he was any more comfortable than we were, riding the 1960-era decrepit bus with its dilapidated seats for miles and hours over unpaved, potholed roads beneath the scorching Indian sun. With the windows of the bus jammed open, allowing no reprieve from dust and choking grime, and the shrill horn-honking accentuating the purgatorial discord, the heat and pollution and noise bore down on him as equally as it did on all of us. Yet he showed no sign of the dissonance with the *what is-ness* of it that I was feeling—that I am sure many of us felt, as we surged from dusty town to dusty town, one swampy roadside restroom and ancient soot-blackened shrine to the next.

With him, there was then, as always, a palpable quality of the simple acceptance of life. Here was an ordinary man, but living within an extraordinary view. From any table in the café, any seat on the bus or airplane, any room in the hotel or dingy hostel, he seemed to have a 360-degree view onto a limitless universe—a vantage point in which all the externals, all the arisings and fallings of phenomena, were no more nor less than what they were—and none of it deterred him from the single point of light that was his love affair with his beloved guru.

This overarching vision, this "other world" view, appeared to imbue the simplest activity with authentic delight for him. From a flea market explored and a treasure found, to a well-made cup of coffee, to a slapstick movie enjoyed, a toothpick offered at the end of a meal, an agreement made and kept by one of his students, an expression of rigorous self-honesty without apologies, a word left unsaid, a beautiful turn of phrase, a gesture devoid of manipulation of others—any of these tapped a well of gracefulness in him that flowed, uncontaminated with sentimentality.

∾

Rewind. **Arrival.**

When our small group of three plus Lee arrived in Chennai from Phoenix, Arizona, it was a full twenty-four hours later, and 1 AM in India. Twenty friends from around the world—Montana, California, Mexico, France, Germany and Romania—stood outside the airport, bright-eyed and eager to greet us, amidst an encampment of vibrant Indians waiting to meet up with their families or friends now stumbling from baggage claim alongside us. Our twenty-three-member international party would form the nucleus of sangha traveling together throughout southern India for the next seventeen days. After hellos and hugs all around, we loaded gear and bodies into two small passenger vans and headed out for what would be a four-hour ride direct to Tiruvannamalai—to Triveni II, Lee's small Indian ashram, which was only a two-minute walking distance from the gates of the Yogi Ramsuratkumar ashram, and our first stop on the trip.

As our vans jettisoned into the night, peeling off from the throngs and the city flickering in the distance behind a veil of dense humidity and smoke, I sat in the jerry-rigged VW bus on a bench seat, back-to-back with the driver and facing my guru, with Jimmy (my old nemesis from Event days) to his right. The wee morning hour, coupled with having passed through umpteen time zones, was so disorienting that I was forced to relax and acclimate. I envisioned Neil Armstrong taking his first steps on the moon: all the training and simulation could not have possibly prepared him for the surge of emotion and sensation in those first moments. Similarly, my senses were making all kinds of autonomous adjustments as I settled in to the new atmosphere of planet India.

The smell of spices flooded my nostrils with the aromas of ginger, turmeric, cardamom, cinnamon, and the more exotic garam masala, along with a powerful infusion of sewage and diesel fumes. This assault to my olfactory senses along with the intestine-liberating bus ride was sufficient to initiate my gag reflex. Then, as if on cue, a graceful breeze carrying an intoxicating perfume of gardenia and night-blooming jasmine eased through the window and, like smelling salts, quenched my urge to purge. Praise Shiva!

India impressions were zooming around me at light speed, and all these sensations were on a collision course with my westernized, homogenized, sanitized reality. There was no turning back as our jitney bus lurched, in the dark of an absent moon, over ancient roads and through some kind of time portal, banking off black holes masquerading as potholes, the combination of which made those first moments a spacewalk, and the ride of my life.

∽

Yogi Ramsuratkumar Ashram, Tiruvannamalai

We arrived at 6 AM. An imposing darshan hall (the Temple) dwarfed a half-dozen self-effacing structures and stood out as the focal point of the ashram. Palm trees, begonia, hibiscus and tulsi bushes scalloped the white-washed buildings that dotted the hard-packed earthen grounds, while female devotees in white cotton saris and men in dhotis worked in intentional silence, sweeping, watering and stirring aromatic pots under the shade of a thatched portico. The exotic cries of peacock, rooster and mourning dove serenaded all as they worked, providing the perfect soundtrack to the serenity of the morning scene.

Our sangha was met by Ma Devaki, Yogi Ramsuratkumar's personal servant for over twenty years. She is an elegant woman with the recognizable English of a Harvard business degree. In her late fifties then, she possessed the warmth of a generous mother and the bearing of a First Lady. Her hair, neatly wrapped in a thick coil at her nape, was the jet-black color that is so customary among Indian women of her age and caste, and her dress was a pure white sari with a simple band of gold brocade at the border, one shoulder draped with a stoneware-colored shawl. Graciously, she greeted Lee with the traditional *Namaste* gesture, then with her arm she waved an embrace to our entire traveling party, indicating for us all to move in closer to her. "Please come—all of you—have your morning coffee. We have coffee ready for you."

"Great!" Lee said with an enthusiasm that unmasked his lust for coffee.

At that, our group migrated to an open-air dining hall with cool cement floors lined with a network of grass mats, falling into single file behind Lee as we neared a long line of tables topped with pots of steaming Indian coffee. Palming our tin cups with both hands, like beggars holding our alms bowls, we graciously accepted the offering of the sweet creamy brew, then circled and milled like cats into a spot on the floor where we would savor that first initiatory cup.

"Breakfast is to be served in an hour's time," Ma said. "There is no rush, and when you have finished, please go to the darshan hall and join the devotees—they have begun the morning chanting."

"Great!" Lee said once again with the same robust enthusiasm. Then he slapped his knees and bounded from his grass mat, striking out across the courtyard of damp earth to the darshan hall. His stride extended to the full reach of his legs, as if he were mindful, even in walking, to use only what was needed. The force of his determination was hard to ignore, signaling to us to finish our coffee and join him.

Inside the darshan hall—constructed of painted white cement, with ceilings that arched fifty feet at the apex—an enormous statue of the Yogi stood twenty-five-feet tall. As is the custom in many traditional Hindu ashrams, men sat on one side and women on the other. The Indian women had begun the chant and, as a group, had taken up the ritual circumambulation of the statue. After about a half hour, the women peeled away and went back to their seats, signaling to the men, who stood in turn and, like the changing of guards, continued circumambulating the statue without breaking the chant until a gong announced that it was time for breakfast.

We returned to the courtyard to find the ashram filled with hundreds of devotees all lining up for the same morning meal. The assembled crowd created a visual feast far more interesting than breakfast proved to be . . . save for the eating with our hands part. It was the women dressed in saris of every color and textile that captivated my attention. Many appeared to be dressed in their best silk, elegantly folded with brocade borders, tucked in symmetrical folds, discrete from shoulder to ankle. Others wore everyday cotton saris that looked to be their only one; these were often tattered and limp and exposed the dark skin of a midriff or back, either fatty or lean. "Modern" women dressed in pajama pants and coordinating kurta tops enhanced with chiffon scarves that flowed down their backs together with their ropes of silken black hair.

Then there was the jewelry! Multicolored bangles up to the elbow; earrings in elaborate hoops of gold; nose rings with chains that swept a cheek and extended over an ear; anklets with bells jangling; toe rings and sparkling jeweled bindi dots pasted between the eyebrows (the location of the "third eye"). The scene was a spectacle of color and texture and mesmerizing beauty.

The women of India are an exotic blend of earthy, elegant and vital, whether shy or outgoing. A compelling combination by any standard. A group of tribal gypsy-looking women caught my eye and waved me over to sit beside them during the chanting. They wore cotton saris, wrapped loosely over their ebony skin. Their hair was wild and dreadlocked, matted gray, and their skin was a weathered patina that spoke of a life of hard work and poverty. Yet, in their faces I read stories of fierce devotion and true freedom. From wide eyes poured an intense blaze indicative of inner radiance, and this dark, unknowable mystery pulled me to them like iron filings to a magnet. Each followed a custom of stretching earlobes with heavy chunks of solid, polished gold that resembled sets of children's building blocks with a hole drilled through the middle. Some wore two, three or four of these gold blocks in the bands of their earlobes, which dangled to their shoulders. Squatting on the ground, hips wide and lower limbs spread like spiders over the earth, they shook tambourines and stomped their ankle bells while their bodies rode the currents of the chant.

I felt a preternatural certainty that these women and I had met somewhere before, but equal certainty that we hadn't. Could they be the tribal Kali worshipers I'd read about? The ones from the Tarini Ma temple of my namesake? And what was *their* connection to Yogi Ramsuratkumar? Questions flooded my mind as my body surrendered to the greater force of the chant, content in the unknowable mystery.

On that cool clay ground in the heat of the Indian sun, as tablā players drove the chant to a roiling pace and these mysterious women abandoned themselves to their fierce devotion, electricity coursed through me so powerfully that I lost sight of myself. Clearly, I was no more nor less than these women. I too was, in that moment, an unknowable mystery, a dark beauty.

Meeting these tribal women was a reunion with the Feminine, that essential substance of Being. With this encounter,

I *knew* that all the money I'd ever spent on clothes or skin regimes was a wasted attempt to replicate in appearance what I felt I lacked in inner substance. As the chanting came to a close, I bowed graciously in their direction, made eye contact, and drifted more deeply into the mood of passionate devotion they had shared with me. Yet, as I rose to leave, I noted that my mind was stuck with a somewhat nagging question: *Where can I get a pair of those gold earrings?*

∿

After meditation on our last day at the Yogi Ramsuratkumar ashram, we were invited by Ma Devaki to join in the ritual of circumambulating the ashram and chanting Yogi Ramsuratkumar's name, as was her private custom every morning. Karla, a woman from our Arizona sangha, approached Ma Devaki with a request. Might she be permitted to wear shoes on the morning walk? she asked, explaining to Ma that she had painful problems with her feet. Although she understood that it was customary to remove shoes on the ashram's sacred ground, would her shoes be permissible? Ma Devaki fixed her kind, kohl-colored eyes on Karla, took hold of both her hands, and said, "Of course—yes—yes. Be free! Bhagwan would have wanted us only to bless and praise, and for you to be free. Please do what you need to take care of yourself."

Any woman could have said the same thing to Karla, so it was not the words Ma chose. It was her embodied context. It was the absence of any hint of piety or New Age rhetoric of *Be free!* Or, what's more, of sentimentality. Ma was a powerful presence who could fill a room, yet what struck me was that she took up no space. Instead, she held open the door for Divine Influence to enter, without encumbering the space with herself.

I witnessed *Woman,* and felt the Feminine pour through that door and enfold Karla in an authentic graciousness.

We left the Yogi Ramsuratkumar ashram that day to head south on our journey to Kanyakumari. On that disharmonic, spine-jarring bus ride I found myself relaxing into the *what is* of India. I quietly observed the miles of rural countryside passing by and, instead of chit-chatting, I directed that energy inward to the Work of observing my mind. There, on that unpadded seat, I entered into the cave of my inner life to observe the arising disappointment that I did not get the spiritual souvenirs I'd imagined I would—like another hit of that intoxicating bliss or the fabled Kundalinī Rising. "After all, aren't these the hallmarks of India? And wouldn't they prove that my practice is producing results?" I heard my mind say. As I observed the content of the dialogue of my mind without judgment, uncensored, these thoughts drifted away as rain clouds eventually do to reveal the sun. Behind these mental concepts, I felt and saw the sun illuminating the reality of *clinging*: clinging to experiences and to appearances, be it aesthetics, clothes, shoes, privacy, health, youthful skin, or ideas. And I saw the variety of clinging known as "spiritual materialism," as Chögyam Trungpa called it—the accumulation of spiritual experiences and the appearances of spiritual realization. "Clinging . . ." I heard myself say out loud as the bus driver leaned on the horn.

FOURTEEN

Untangling the Roots of Love

Roots are not in landscape or a country, or a people, they are inside you.

—ISABEL ALLENDE

"*B*e that which nothing can take root in" was a teaching and a practice that Lee shared with his students ages ago. The poetry of it hooked me right away with the alluring possibility to be such loamy soil that no tenacious weeds of knarly egos—mine or others'—would sink their roots into me.

The practice, as appealing as it was, was flat-out impossible. So whenever I heard it, I filed it in my Spiritual Koan To Do file. The impossibility of it was like when I was a kid and my mom would say, "Eat your broccoli, there are starving kids in

India." I'd feel for those kids in India, I did. But what was my eating my broccoli going to do to help them? I'd roll my eyes in resignation and put the message in the What Moms Say file, as I simultaneously filed my broccoli in my napkin.

Although I haven't personally done a deep dive on this "be nothing" consideration (because I figured I had enough on my spiritual practice plate), I have given it a thought or two. Might this be one of those tricky slogans that Tibetan monks meditate on for fourteen years in a cave, after which they emerge enlightened, make a cup of yak tea, and *presto chango* are whisked off to their Buddha nature? Then I inquired: Seriously, what is being something that nothing can take root in really like? Air? CO_2 gas? Or maybe it's like interpretive dance, loose and spontaneous, unchoreographed, sort of? Despite my having pretty much resigned myself to failure before I even got started, the practice resurfaced when my dear friend Linda got cancer.

"In a large community gathering years ago, I asked Lee for some help with my anger with my husband," Linda said. "I told him I was so frustrated I felt like I was choking, and I needed help working with how to manage these feelings about Stan." All eighty-nine pounds of her lay stretched on the Barcalounger that engulfed what was left of her. Her emaciated arm dangled, scrawny as a chicken wing and hooked up to a titanium syringe thingamabob (some kinda sci-fi freaky shit) that fed radioactive dye into her veins. The dye was intended to light up any remaining cancer in her body, like the Las Vegas Strip at night, and the PET scan to follow would capture their image. The scan was to be the moment of truth, the report card that would tell her the results of a seven-week course of toxic radiation and chemotherapy treatments that we all hoped had taken the cancer away with what it took of her body. "Do you know what he said to me?" Linda continued, with her Kentucky piss-and-vinegar attitude still larger than life.

Linda has been married to that guitar-playing Jesus-doppelgänger guy Stan for forty-some years. That same guy I'd met so many years ago in The Event. The pair of them, twenty-something years as students of our guru, are some of my very best friends to this day. I love to get Linda whomped up in telling stories of the "old days" of the sangha, relating all the radical antics of our young spiritual master. But on this day I only wanted to hear Linda's stories to take my mind, and hers, off the PET scan. So I egged her on a wee bit more than usual.

"Lay it on me, Linda Louski, I'm all ears! What did the big guy say next?"

"He said, '*You* be that which nothing can take root in.' He may as well have said, 'Go bake some cookies.' I stared at him speechless, as if to say, 'What? Couldn't I do some Kegel exercises or recite a mantra, or do you have a Plan B?'"

"Did he have a Plan B?" I asked.

"*Nothing!* He just looked at me with that shit-eatin' grin of his, as if to say, 'If you have a better idea, Linda, by all means, go for it.'" She picked up her cup and drank a few sips of water to rehydrate.

A Kentucky-born spitfire, Linda weaves a wicked yarn with Southern flair made completely of non sequiturs. One has to pay close attention when she's on a roll. No radioactive dye was going to slow her down, and I was not about to advise her to rest up so I could play catch up.

After another sip or two of water she was rehydrated and ready with another story. "Then, there was the time I was in the ashram kitchen cooking during a community celebration while Lee gave a talk in the next room. I could hear him over the speaker system telling a story that involved me, and he was telling the story all wrong," she said, as she scooched up in her seat, took another sip of her water, and then tucked a blanket around herself the way a mother tucks her child in. Then she went on: "He was *making shit up* to make the story more interesting! I was furious with him as I listened, but I chose to finish what I was doing in the kitchen and to approach him the next day at his desk. That's when I accused him of lying." Linda caught her breath again.

"As soon as I said those words, 'You lied, Lee,' a look came over his face as if to say 'You win!' I was crushed by his look, realizing instantly what I'd done. Instead of allowing the guru to use me to illustrate a teaching lesson for us all, I made being right and winning more important. In that moment, I swore never to forget that look on his face and that I would never again try to win with the guru. I came here for help from the guru, and the guru came here to help me win over my ego," she said.

"Did you keep that promise to yourself?" I asked, as I stood up to get her more water.

"Yes, I believe I have," she said. Immediately she launched into another story, this one about a time when Lee had made a big salad for dinner for everyone. As the food was being passed around, suddenly he yelled out, 'Pass *that one there* to Linda,' as he pointed intently at a smaller, separate bowl. She was confused at first, then Lee clarified by asking her, "Aren't you the one who wrote me a note asking not to have vinegar on your salad, or did you lie to me?" Although Linda hadn't written him a note asking for the favor, the tenderness of his gesture in preparing a special salad for someone was not lost on her. He was mistaken, but she remembered her vow, to allow the guru to win.

"I silently agreed to receive what he was offering—the salad and the teaching lesson," Linda concluded softly.

At first blush Linda's stories seemed to be plucked randomly from the basket of her long-term relationship with Lee, but after hearing them aloud we both noticed a hidden treasure. In each story was an object lesson provided by Lee (consciously or not), where the true cost of our insistence on being right and winning with others was exposed for what it is: a barrier to the love we profess to want, and to the annihilation of ego that would lead to our "love-tamed heart." In Linda's own case, seeing the look of genuine disappointment on Lee's face, on the previous occasion when she had accused him of lying, had left an indelible mark sufficient for her to feel the pain of remorse that led to untangling the roots of her anger and enabling her to "be that which nothing can take root in."

Just then the nurse broke through the door of our little refuge to take her to her PET scan. Linda stood and took off her fleece hat, exposing a thin, downy regrowth of her previously uprooted hair and looking to me every bit a Tibetan monk sans the saffron robes. I offered a reassuring smile as she left with the nurse.

∽

Dream: I'm tending a rooftop garden—it's filled with a wide variety of tropical trees, palms, bananas and exotic orchids and with tables of vegetable starts and herbs in trays. I look up from something I'm tending to see my guru standing across the greenhouse, squarely facing me. Though he was not a tall man, in the dream he stands statuesque and is holding one tulsi plant—*osmium sanctum*—in each upturned palm, the roots tangled, dirty and dangling between each of his ten fingers. I'm conscious, in the dream state, that my guru is dead—though, as is the gift of dreams, he seems ever more alive. I stop what I'm doing, walk over to him, drop to my knees in front of him and bow at his feet, shedding tears of gratitude.

When I woke from the dream I was aware of Lee being in and around me, aware also of the significance of the tulsi plants he held—they are revered as one of the highest classes of medicines in the Ayurvedic herbal tradition and known as the "wish-fulfilling tree" in India. My guru standing firmly on the earth holding the tulsi starts, their roots liberated in his hands, symbolized for me the wish for liberation from the illusion of separation, and showed me a human being who *was that* which nothing can take root in.

In his book *Before the Sun*, John Mann quotes his teacher Rudi instructing him in the meaning behind an Indian saying: "A human being is a seed. You plant him in the earth and he sprouts. But a teacher is a scorched seed. You plant him in the earth and nothing happens." Rudi then goes on to explain:

> A human being is constantly creating more karma for himself . . . You put a seed in the earth and something sprouts. There is no end to it. But a teacher is someone who has been through life and is no longer attached to it. He has been scorched by his experience and no longer sprouts. It is then, and only then, that a spiritual force can exert a gentle but continuous influence.

No sooner had Linda slipped behind the door to have her PET scan than, like the ordinary seed Rudi mentions, my thoughts started sprouting fears: "What if the report doesn't look good?" "What if she has to do more chemo?" "What if Linda dies?" My thoughts were roots searching for a place in me to take hold and spiral out, separating me from what was real and from my ability to be present with Linda.

Then I turned my attention to my guru's instruction, "Be that which nothing can take root in," recalling how just one look from him was all it took and Linda was forever changed by letting the guru win. In so doing, maybe she too had been "scorched"—the way Rudi claimed a teacher was—by experience. Maybe some seed of karma had been eliminated for her, the way the chemo is supposed to scorch the seeds of cancer so they no longer sprout. *What if?* I asked myself.

Linda's PET scan came back cancer free. "Be that which nothing can take root in," I said to myself. Some months later I learned that my guru had cancer; another opportunity calling me to practice "Be that which nothing can take root in." My guru died. "Be that which nothing can take root in."

There is a salutation in Hindi: *Jai Guru*. It is an expression of gratitude for the guru and, more specifically, a declaration: *May the guru be victorious over illusion*. When we say "Jai Guru," we are not speaking about the person of the guru, but petitioning that his or her purpose prevail; that he or she be triumphant in helping all those who want to be a scorched seed, liberated from everything that separates us, even our sacred notions of liberation, and receive the guru's ultimate gift of love.

FIFTEEN

The Death of My True Guru

Let sorrowful longing dwell in your heart,
never giving up, never losing hope.
The Beloved says, "The broken ones are My Darlings."
Crush your heart, be broken.

—*NOBODY SON OF NOBODY: POEMS OF SHAIKH ABU
SAEED ABIL-KHEIR,* RENDITION BY VRAJE ABRAMIAN

"Do you know how bad it is out there? Do you?" Lee's raspy blues voice railed between low wails from the guitar during a particularly juicy rendition of "All Along the Watchtower," a signature classic of Bob Dylan's. Heads bobbed, hips gyrated, and the packed house swayed in unison, rocking the room in rhythm with the Delta blues. The sultry guitar and rolling backbeat of the drums continued as my guru, the lead singer in the band, howled again, "No, you don't know!" as he raised the volume to a roar. "YOU DON'T KNOW THE HALF OF IT. If you did, you wouldn't be smiling. It's bad, and it's gunna get worse!" Lee seemed to be calling for some response with each roar. As he goaded, broader grins carved across the faces of the crowd, registering who among us was gettin' what he was puttin' down. The floor beneath our feet rumbled.

I was one of those smug cats grinning and gyrating, as images of tsunamis, refugees in camps, economies crashing and climate change all flashed through my mind. Certainly *I* registered his meaning, validating in my mind that *I* knew what he was asking.

But why this discordant downer now? I wondered. Why remind me how bad it is "out there" in the middle of this red-hot blues set goin' on here? I came here to lose myself to the blues, to sweat till my body was glazed and my loins were oiled. Jeezus Lee, you get me all warmed up, then pour a bucket of cold water on my head? Can't you just sing the goddamn blues and leave me to my illusions for one blissful evening?

My guru, with his dreadlocks down to his knees, covered in tattoos, was a radical contradiction: a rock n' roll and blues man, a hopeless romantic, a lover of cheesy movies, a "bad poet" (by his own admission), a slave to his own beloved guru, and a bodhisattva, all at once. He used music, theater, sacred art, graffiti, tattoos—whatever means possible—to preserve the dharma and the possibility of communicating objective beauty in his lifetime, and ours, in a world filled with abject suffering, and ignorance of how bad it is.

∽

"I am choosing to live, not choosing not to die," he announced in a communication that went out broadly to the entire sangha, from America to Canada, France, Germany, India and Mexico, and other dots around the globe. This was the context he held regarding his diagnosis of cancer, and he expected us, as mature practitioners, to hold this context, too. Knowing this, we each did our best to respect his wishes and to manage our various emotions about his health—to align with his context.

In May of 2010, although I knew (but would not admit) that my guru was living his very last days (in fact, he had only six months remaining), I asked if I might meet up with him and his family while they were in Paris that summer. "I'll be in Amsterdam on business while you all are in France. I could . . . ," I said.

"Sure! Great! Make the arrangements with Sharon. I'd love to see you there," he said.

The plan was to meet him in Paris for a quick visit—a day of sacred-art shopping—then head to the outskirts of the city where we would link up with a group of French sangha who were planning a meal and a gathering with others in his family. I had arrived in Paris one day prior. In the St. Germaine district, near the Saint-Sulpice church, two blocks from the Luxembourg Palace, I had spent the day exploring the grand gardens, took a stroll to the Louvre, and finished off by traipsing back through charming rues lined with cafés, stopping now and then for a little window shopping along the way.

The next morning, as scheduled, his van pulled up at the corner of Pl. Saint-Sulpice and Rue Bonaparte at 9:30. Lee was at the wheel, as always, and no sooner was my luggage loaded than the door slammed shut—*whap!* He sped away from the curb as if we were being chased by Interpol. Once inside the van, greetings were exchanged all around with others in his traveling party, and small talk volleyed forward and back. Lee, however, dispensed no talk, intent on navigating the chaos of Paris streets and preserving his cancer-ravaged mouth for more important communications.

"Which lane, which lane?" he shouted.

"Right, right—you turn right at the next light!" Sharon bellowed above the din of city traffic.

"It'd be nice if I didn't hafta ask," he said, growling back and giving her the cue that he expected to rely on her paying attention. Sharon said nothing in reply, but shifted her focus quickly to navigating, not socializing. We were headed to a movie theater near the Champs Élysées, where we would pick up a few others, then shoot to the Sorbonne where all the children and half of our adult group would unload to spend their afternoon touring the famous university and nearby cafés.

As we made the drop-off at a charming roundabout lined with shops, someone asked if I'd like to go on the tour with the kids or stay with Lee and the two others who would visit art dealers with him.

"Thanks, but I'd like to stay with Lee, given the choice. I'm only here two days, and I'd like to spend them in his company," I said.

Back in the van with Mary and Sharon and with Lee at the wheel, I slipped into the seat behind him. Throughout the excitement and hustle I was acutely aware of how emaciated my guru had become since I'd seen him just two months ago. His once Rubenesque physique was now wasted, his once glorious dreadlocks long since shaved to a stubble. Previously striking features were shadows at death's door, and his distinctive voice of gravel and gravitas had been stripped by tongue cancer. He coughed a moist, frequent and painful-sounding cough; his words, when he did speak, were a guttural jumble too heartbreaking to bear. I'll never forget the moments of that first impression. Refraining from small talk, restrained, I did my level best not to show the shock I felt, although, as always, I didn't believe I was concealing anything from him.

Once the driving coordinates were clear and we came to a stop at a relatively calm intersection, I caught his eyes slicing a direct stare into the rearview mirror and fixed on me. In the galaxies of those eyes that I'd come to love, the whites that used to frame the vivid glacial-blue were now a frame of jaundice yellow.

"It's great to see you," he said, straining to enunciate each word so that I naturally leaned closer to the back of his head, while never breaking eye contact with him in the mirror.

"It's really great to see you, too," I said, beaming a smile shaped by a depth of gratitude for which I have no other reference point than him, and the unsettling knowledge, beyond my understanding, that this moment of gazing in the mirror would be our final darshan.

"That is because you are a *great devotee*," he boomed, leaning hard on the "great devotee" part. His delivery felt to me as if he were singing the blues—filled with a heartbreak and beauty and plea for human dignity. Then he broke eye contact and sped away into the chaos of Paris streets.

My guru never says anything he does not mean, and he always—always—means what he says. This is something I have come to trust in him with impeccability, even if I've never been willing to radically rely on or obey. That he uttered the words "because you are a great devotee," at a time when words were at a premium, rocked me back on my heels. Were I standing next to him, I'm convinced I would have needed to regain my balance. The moment the comment was out of my guru's mouth, however, my mind showed up as reliably as Pavlov's dog, and cranked on AM Self-Doubt Talk Radio—*You talkin' to me, Lee?*—as my head all but swiveled around my cervical spine to look at the nobody-else behind me. Then, like uninvited guests, the panel of self-doubting and self-deprecating experts inside my mind all began talking at once: "What have you been smoking, Lee?" "NEWS FLASH, Big Guy. I'm the one running away whenever you come to town? I probably wouldn't be sitting here now if I wasn't scared shitless that you're dying; scareder still that, had I been in Europe so close and hadn't made this effort to get here, I'd live with regret. I'm sure you noticed that I took my sweet time strolling the streets of Paris, window shopping and visiting the Louvre, before I dragged my sorry ass into this cruel van with you, didn't you?"

About then, my Inner Devotee teamed up with my Knowing Wise Woman to turn down the white noise, despite the imagined "facts." I was humbled, leveled really, both from the shock of his physical decline and the radiance gushing from his being, undaunted by death. I managed to nod a bobble-headed recognition, and smiled back at him.

While he blazed a trail through Paris, helter-skelter in search of art dealers he knew, Sharon, Mary and I hung on for the ride. He navigated one-lane cobblestone streets, darting in and out of rue this and rue that, as Sharon shouted cues to the next "X" on the map. Then he would screech to a halt, necks whiplashing our heads back in place. Lee and Sharon would leap from the van before it came to what felt like a complete stop, and the two of them would disappear into some hole-in-the-wall artifact shop in the back alley. Mary would slide to take the wheel while I jumped forward to shotgun, like the getaway crew in a diamond heist. We'd double park, if need be, or be forced to circle around the block to be on our mark the minute Lee and Sharon emerged. We had to save time and make it to the next dealer before the sun went down! Lee would assume the wheel, we'd take our assigned seats, and away we'd go, lurching into the din of Paris roundabouts, horns bleating, sirens blaring, people shuffling. Then, a jubilant Lee would recant the story of a "great deal" or what kind of "worthless crap" he'd found, all joyous and guttural and snarl.

This madcap scene replayed itself a half-dozen times, and we three women fell down the rabbit hole, reluctantly, but complicit in a strange way with this crazy Baul's adventures and misadventures. What kind of madness was *this*? What kind of crazy talk to have him call me a "great devotee"? After all, I was the one who smoked hash in Amsterdam and drank hundred-dollar bottles of wine, having misplaced my practice probably somewhere in Kansas.

During those three short days, I felt myself at once grasping at the moments in a desperate attempt to stop time and rewind the clock, and still hiding. He graciously invited me to sit near him during a meal, as was his custom whenever I found the time in my busy schedule to be with him. As we exchanged small talk about my work, and my eyes met his penetrating gaze, I felt a haunting sense of déjà vu. It was as if he and I had been seated together for eons, lost to all but the other. In those few seconds I was transported outside of time and space, like the two lovers in Gustav Klimt's famous painting *The Kiss*. One kiss suspended these lovers in a cocoon of cosmic geometry and generative blooms, like a spiraling helix of ultimate truth and universal beauty. Lee's eyes transformed into time portals through which an unfathomable radiance of Being shot through the cracks in my fear, resistance, shame, self-doubt and hatred to shatter all illusion. Lee had gone. He was altogether gone, "gone beyond" as the Heart Sutra reminded. My favorite among his poems detached from my memory and looped around inside me, like the reciting of my mantra on each bead of my prayer mala:

> I don't need hashish
> I smoke my Father's Rags
> and stagger off
> lost to all but He
> I am drunk—
> blind and deaf
> to the pleas
> of the sober.

I wasn't stoned. But maybe his comment "That is because you are a great devotee!" transmitted to me as he sped like a wild man, completely mad, through the streets of Paris was a kiss filled with second-hand smoke from the pipe in which he smoked his Father's rags. Maybe I'd already inhaled his intoxicating devotion, and I was desperately hooked and he was just reminding me that there was no turning back, before he stumbled off drunk, lost in his great devotion to his guru, blind and deaf to the sobering pleas of death.

❧

November 16, 2010, on my way from Prescott to Phoenix for a work week there. I was exactly five miles from the ashram, in my car, when my cell phone rang. "Hello?"

"Tarini, I'm calling to let you know Lee passed this morning around 5 AM." I recognized the voice of a long-time friend from the sangha without him needing to identify himself. "I'm calling everyone to let them know. His body will be prepared and in the darshan hall by tomorrow, where you can come see him, chant, and sit with him over the next couple days," he said. "Where are you now?"

"I'm in my car headed to Phoenix for a business trip."

"Okay, travel safe," he said.

"Thank you for the call," I said, and we hung up. I pulled to the side of the road. I wept.

In the days that followed, sangha flew in from all corners of the world to pay homage to their beloved guru. Other teachers, gurus, and lamas wrote letters or came to pay their respects, too. There was a great celebration—with smiles, chanting, singing, feasting and tears, but no wailing. All was held in the good, shared company of devotees bound to one another by the love and respect for a true guru.

Arnaud Desjardins, an octogenarian and a great hero of "the Work," a man for whom Lee had the greatest of admiration and love, came from France to honor his dharma brother. Speaking to the assembled sangha and guests about his experience of communion upon viewing Lee's body, he left us all with an exquisite summation of our teacher, reflecting on the passing of a truly rare human being:

Everything which had made the Lee one could describe, all that prompted admiration or criticism, all the specificities of his "crazy wisdom"—provocation, rock bands and tours, tattoos, trips in the worst conditions, and everyone will add to this list in accordance with his or her own memories—all that has been erased and the universal dimension, "beyond the beyond," was timelessly ruling. Just like a genius painter lays down his brushes, colors and easel, Lee had laid down all the "skillful means" which he had had at his disposal to "rock the ground whereon these sleepers be" . . . Let the peace beyond description emanating from Lee's impressive face, so much more alive than dead, reign now within our hearts...

SIXTEEN

You Cannot Make This Shit Up!

Reality is contradictory. And it's paradoxical.

—Tom Robbins

As I write this chapter I am holed up at my neighbor's home, two miles up the road from my own, on a tiny island with less than 900 inhabitants. When I moved to this island I took a vacation from the dharma, isolated myself from sangha, and I'd have bet good money on the odds that there wasn't a soul around who gave two hoots about seeking refuge in the three jewels: guru, dharma or sangha. The neighbors whose home I am now borrowing have served as profound reminders for me that there is no such thing as a vacation on the path. Had I made that bet, I'd have lost it all.

These are not just *any* neighbors, however. And their home is not just *any* home! My neighbors turned out to be John Mann and his wife Capella. The very same John Mann who wrote *Rudi: 14 Years with My Teacher*, the one that fueled the crazy notion in my dyslexic noggin that I might one day write a book about *my* years with my teacher . . . my crazy teacher who had inspired me to write *this book*.

The Mann's home is more sanctuary than residence, with a collection of sacred art to rival a museum's. In every room, in every corner, at every turn, I am greeted by stone, bronze and silks from Tibet and India. In the morning, I pay my respects to a four-foot-tall Ganesh who reminds me of the value of humility, and of the need to ask for help if I am going to sustain myself on the journey. A three-foot Hanuman on bended knee, chest torn open to reveal his heart, which bears the name of God, is for me the supreme symbol of a great devotee. A six-foot-high wooden Krishna stands in the corner of the living room playing his flute—and I pretend to shape-shift from mere mortal to his love-struck gopi, dancing the legendary Ras Lila with him in the night. Avolakiteshvara and a magnificent poly-headed, thousand-armed Heruka and his consort face me at the desk where I write, sipping hot tea and looking out at the morning sunrise over the Puget Sound as sailboats drift, cedars sway, and clouds disperse above the water, a caramel-crusted glaze. Medicine Buddha, Mahakala and Durga are at my back. Vishnu—considered the preserver of the holy trinity of Hindu gods, along with Brahma the creator and Shiva the destroyer—each sit beside me, holding me in place as I work, helping me create and then destroying whatever does not serve. Spiritual literature that spans every tradition and includes every authentic teacher I've ever read, or hoped to read, lines bookshelves, or is stacked on tables or the floor, like a pantry well stocked with my favorite comfort foods. Buddhism—Vajrayana and Zen—Sufism, Hinduism, Mystical Christianity and Native American . . . all are represented here. Rudi, Da Free John, Krishnamurti, Khyentse Rinpoche, Ramana Maharshi, Nityananda, Thomas Merton, and even my own teacher, Lee Lozowick, are here, near the poets I can never get enough of: Rumi, Hafiz, Kabir and Blake. I am in exalted company, in a home lived in and loved by two great devotees of human potential and, indeed, transformation.

"Tarini, you and Capella must know each other. Have you two met yet?" Ryan said.

Ryan is the local wine steward and French tutor; my tutor who attempted, briefly, to teach me French for my work in Canada and the one person I'd met on the island since I arrived two years prior. He'd invited me to come to a Friday evening wine tasting, held at a local home with an impressive collection of wines.

Capella, the woman I was about to meet, had a beautiful, untamed mane of gray with blond streaks. She wore an ensemble of oranges, purples and pinks, a mix of plaids and floral as I recall, blended in such a way that, on her, worked. Capella's presence in the room stood out in relief against gentrified wainscoting and wooden floors. There was no mistaking this woman for the crone that she was. Either an artist or a thespian, I had guessed. In any case, I knew I wanted to meet her.

"I've not had the pleasure," I said.

"Capella, meet Tarini; Tarini, meet Capella," Ryan obliged. We made eye contact, clinked our wine glasses and toasted.

"Tarini, you have to see Capella's house," Ryan said, as he continued, gushing with enthusiasm. "She has amazing art, similar to yours. Lots of Buddhas and Indian pieces."

"Oh, no kidding, you collect Indian art, Capella?" I pressed to learn more, my curiosity shifting into gear.

"Oh, my husband does, mostly," she said with a dismissive tone, as if to say, "Oh, those dusty old things."

"Capella's husband is very interesting," Ryan added. "He is an author of several spiritual books. I have a hunch you'd like to meet him, too."

"No kidding? What kind of spiritual books does your husband write?"

"Oh, well, he's written several." She paused to sip her wine, then added, "Nothing you would have heard of, though."

"Try me. Like what, for instance?" As a sales professional, I am trained in the discovery process and in asking values-based questions. With every question I asked and Capella answered, I was discovering that our values were lined up like planets in an auspicious configuration.

"Oh, well, one of his better-known books is about his life with his spiritual teacher, called *Rudi: 14 Years with My Teacher*," she said, as she casually plucked a nut from the bar and popped it into her mouth. Turning back to face me and reengage our conversation, she could see my mouth hanging open in amazement, and to both our surprise, tears were rolling in streams down my cheeks. Her casual comment was beginning to sink in: her husband must be John Mann! *Wait. What?* My mind was attempting to catch up to what it was registering.

"John Mann . . . John Mann . . . is your husband?" I said, my eyes now transfixed on hers. She appeared slightly embarrassed, as the small group of locals had turned their attention on us. I removed my glasses to wipe tears from my cheeks, then, on impulse, despite the attention we were getting, wrapped my arms around her as if reuniting with a long-lost sister. She graciously received my hug.

"Do you know of him? Do you know the book?" she said.

"Oh, my gosh!" I stammered. "That book was a turning point in my life with *my* spiritual master."

"Who is your teacher?" she asked.

I told her.

"Lee Lozowick? From Arizona?" Now *she* was open-mouthed.

"Yes, do you know him?"

"Yes, of course we know him. How is he?"

"He died three years ago."

Capella became silent, taking in the news. Then, quietly, reflecting: "Oh. I didn't know. John and I came to dinner at Lee's invitation, to the ashram, on a couple of occasions when we were in Arizona." A longer pause. "Wow, you have to come by our place. You have to meet John. He would love to meet you."

"Yes . . . I would be honored . . . I'd love that . . . I can't believe . . . ? What are the chances . . . ? You couldn't make this up, could you?" I was gushing. Capella laughed, then smiled and nodded, letting me know she knew exactly what I meant.

I had bolted out of Arizona for a self-inflicted "time-out" soon after my guru died, having made both a conscious and metaphoric choice to move to an island, which I am now convinced was some kind of karmic crazy shit or other; call it what you will. But John Mann? My new neighbor? Of all the characters life could have tossed into my path . . . this is straight-up shit you just cannot make up. *Get the hell out—are you freakin' kidding?*

Meeting John Mann and his wife Capella was a mystical shove out of that empty corner of my time-out. Finding John as my neighbor shone a beacon of light on the shore where I had marooned my incompletes. This illumination was not from anything he said or did, but by the sheer magic of his presence—made palpable by a lifetime of devotion to his own and others' transformation, long after his teacher died. John himself was a witness to my own reason for stepping onto the path in the first place—which was for *my* spiritual well-being, not Lee's. Shockingly, I had been operating as if Lee's physical death brought an end to the path. As if his being gone was a permission slip for me to exit and descend from the mountain that is the guru-devotee relationship before I'd made the vertical climb to the summit of its potential.

The *real perils* of the guru-devotee relationship, I am now persuaded, show up after the teacher dies. This is a time in the student's life when he or she must graduate and live the teaching without the often-complicated physical company of the master. For me, to have met a true guru and become his student was something like the karmic Wheel of Fortune hitting my number. To have wasted this winning ticket would have been a tragedy of real consequence. As my sales mentor had said to me so many years ago, "Suck it up, Tarini, and do your job!"

∽

About a year after meeting John and Capella, I learned that my old friend Sundari lived on Orcas Island—the island I could see across the water; the island right next door to mine!

"Hello, Sundari, I mean Sherri, this is Tarini," I said in response to her "Hello" as she answered my call.

"Tarini formerly known as Kristen?" she asked, beaming a smile I could feel.

"Yes, the very same," I replied, as the rainbow of my smile arched through the phone to greet hers.

"Wow! What a wonderful surprise. How long has it been since God's Garden?" she said.

"I think it's going on twenty years."

"Crap, do we have some catching up to do! It is so good to hear your voice."

"Yours too. No kidding? . . . Who knew? . . . We live on neighboring islands! You just can't make this shit up, can you?"

Sundari laughed out loud. Her familiar joyous laugh took me back to God's Garden, and to that pivotal moment when she lovingly shoved me from the superficial cushion of bliss. That impetus from her led me to this treacherous path of taking refuge in the guru, dharma, and sangha, and the very real possibility of being saved from enlightenment.

SEVENTEEN

After Words

When you are ready to slow down *out there* so you can speed up *in here* . . . well, *welcome!*

—LEE LOZOWICK

*L*ee's apparently casual, but gracious, comment noted here was made to me nearly fourteen years ago. His words now shimmer with the intuitive wisdom and the overriding relaxation that characterized his work with me from the get-go. The statement was an affirmation that I had indeed made my way to this path, and it was just a matter of time before I would exhaust my need for the outer appearance of things and dedicate myself to living the dharma, thus giving myself to my heart's longing. That recognition, when it occurred, would swing wide the door to *his* world!—that ultimately real existence I'd longed for.

I finished this book on the isolated southeastern edge of the big island of Hawaii in Puna: an island within an island made by lava flows that have limited access to only one road in and the same one out. This place is unlike any other I've lived in because it is a volcanic and visceral reminder of the urgency for tending to my inner life and for taking refuge in the dharma. There is a Bible scripture from my childhood that has resurfaced here, one in which Paul admonishes the Philippians in a letter he wrote after Jesus had died. "Work out your own salvation with fear and trembling," he said.

Roughly six months before Lee died, he spoke to a group of students in a vein reminiscent of Paul's admonishment during a talk in Bozeman, Montana: "If you are thinking of me on your death bed, you've missed the whole point. Better get with the program, folks." I was not in the room when these words were said, but, reading them later, their impact on me was like the enduring memory of Paul's unsentimental memo. Lee similarly served us, students and devotees alike, with his no-frills reminder that he was not then, nor was he ever, a *savior.* That we had better cut the apron strings of immature dependency on the man—Lee—and install the dharma he taught at the center of our lives. "You are each responsible adults—grow up and do your own work!" If I heard him say this once, I heard it countless times throughout his life with us. Yes, I affirm; I am responsible. I am the stand for my own sageness, Lee. Neither you nor anyone else is going to save me, nor tend to my own soul's well-being.

This place in which I find myself, on this Hawaiian island, is rooted in tradition, family, and self-identity expressed through

Aloha! The word in Hawaiian is used like "hello" or "good-bye," but it extends far beyond a salutation of good will. This expression actually reflects an awareness that is ingrained in the people who live in this place—a land where five of the most active volcanoes in the world have erupted since . . . well, forever! A near-constant flow of molten lava rises up from the earth here when and where it chooses, leveling homes or businesses, stripping away possessions and dreams, and tearing at the fabric of the illusion of permanence. *Aloha* is an affirmation, a call to action for each human being to step forward on the path of unity and harmony with his or her *real self*, with others as they are, and with God. It encapsulates a dharma of kindness, patience, and humility. In short, *Aloha* actually means "God in us," and therefore celebrates the dharma in the midst of the impersonal actions of nature.

Here, where the vast blue sea meets Pelé's volcanic feminine force, flowing unobstructed and paving the way to a new earth, I cannot help but be reminded of Kali with her black skin and flailing fury of hair, wielding her blade that cuts through illusion and paves the way to an enlightened view of the laws of nature. I come full circle back to that dark mystery, to the fierce sword of great devotion in the steady hand of practice that cuts through all clinging, to reveal that "mind is luminous," as the Buddha said. I am back at the beginning, leaning into the work my true guru gave me to do: to choose a life of steadfast practice for its intrinsic reward of dignity and nobility, of *God in us*. In this great task I have the help of the dharma and of my sangha and of all my friends who kindly call me to step forward on the path to embody my real self.

This morning, as I sat for my daily practice of meditation on the deck atop a wide swath of lava, my senses were bombarded.

I could hear the rhythmic sound of the ocean pounding the jagged spine of the coast only a block away, while palm leaves chattered softly behind me in a cool morning breeze that carried notes of jasmine and plumeria. I could taste the hint of salt on my lips and felt the heat of the sun reflected off the glistening black rocks as it warmed my skin. The assault sent me back to my childhood; to the countless summer days spent blissfully lost to all, at the edge of the ocean, wisely innocent in the presence of God, and of *me in Thee*. Then my mind shifted from memory to marveling at the journey that had brought me here to this impermanent edge of the world, to this place of such jewel-like beauty and harsh uncertainty, just like this path of refuge that my longing led me to. I rejoiced at the good fortune to have met a true guru who graciously helped me see *my* enlightenment, even my insights and indeed all experience, for not more nor less than what it is. Tears flowed up and out from a deep well of gratitude for the magic and mystery of it all; of me, an unlikely devotee, stumbling along this uneven path of devotion, evermore humbled by all that I see. T.S. Eliot captured it best in his poem "Little Gidding" when he wrote, "We shall not cease from exploration / And the end of all our exploring / Will be to arrive where we started / And know the place for the first time."

Recommended Reading

Caplan, Mariana. *Eyes Wide Open: Cultivating Discernment on the Spiritual Path*. Sounds True, 2009.

Caplan, Mariana. *Halfway Up the Mountain: The Error of Premature Claims to Enlightenment*, Kindle Edition. Hohm Press, 2014.

Khyentse, Dzongsar Jamyang. *What Makes You Not a Buddhist*. Shambhala, 2008.

Lozowick, Lee. *The Alchemy of Transformation*. Hohm Press, 1996.

Mann, John. *Before The Sun: Meeting Rudi*. Createspace, 2014.

Mann, John. *Rudi: 14 Years with My Teacher*. Rudra, 2001. Only used copies available online.

Red Hawk. *Self Observation: The Awakening of Conscience*. Hohm Press, 2009.

Ryan, Regina Sara. *The Woman Awake: Feminine Wisdom for Spiritual Life*. Hohm Press, 1998.

Sell, Christina. *Yoga from the Inside Out*. Hohm Press, 2003.

Trungpa Rinpoche, Chögyam. *Cutting Through Spiritual Materialism*. Shambhala Classics, 2002.

Permissions

The publisher and the author wish to thank:

Coleman Barks for the generosity of his work on behalf of all, and for his kind permission in allowing us to use his translations of Rumi and Bawa Muhaiyaddeen from the book: *The Illuminated Prayer: The Five-Times Prayer of the Sufis,* by Coleman Barks, illustrations by Michael Green (Ballantine Books, 2000).

Robert Bly for his permission to use an excerpt (quoted here on page 86) from *The Kabir Book: Forty-Four of the Ecstatic Poems of Kabir, Versions by Robert Bly* (Beacon Press, 1993).

About the Author

Tarini Bauliya was a buckskin-wearing naturalist, a fitness guru, a model, and an insecure single mother before she met her spiritual teacher, the American-born Lee Lozowick. *Saved from Enlightenment* is her memoir, recounting how this traditional guru "saved" her—a hippie-chic turned national sales manager for a major health products company—from the trap of a dead-end spiritual search.

Tarini has been published in spiritual journals, and currently does sales consultation and freelance writing on such topics as marketing, health, wellness and natural medicine. She teaches "Story-Selling"©—the art of transforming sellers and buyers into values-aligned peers who work together on behalf of consumers. She lives on an organic farm in the Pacific Northwest—sans buckskins.

About Hohm Press

Hohm Press is committed to publishing books that provide readers with alternatives to the materialistic values of the current culture and promote self-awareness, the recognition of interdependence and compassion. Our subject areas include religious studies, natural health, parenting, women's issues, the arts and poetry. We are proud to offer the work of contemporary spiritual teachers Lee Lozowick, Arnaud Desjardins, Robert Frager and Taisen Deshimaru, and to present books by authors distinguished in their fields: Georg and Brenda Feuerstein (Yoga and Tantric Studies), Philippe Coupey and Richard Collins (Zen Buddhism), Claudio Naranjo (Enneagram), Mariana Caplan (Religious Studies), Red Hawk (poetry and self-observation), and Vraje Abramian (poetic translations).

www.hohmpress.com
hppublisher@cableone.net
928-636-3331
800-321-2700